HISTORY

OF

COMPANY K.

1ST (INFT,) PENN'A RESERVES

by H. N. Minnigh

THOMAS PUBLICATIONS
Gettysburg, PA 17325

Captain H. N. Minnigh.
Standing before members of Company K in June of 1863.

The Company K monument is located on the southwest quadrant of Lincoln Square, Gettysburg. The top center plaque reads:

Company K
First Pennsylvania Reserves
(Thirtieth Regiment)
First (McCandless') Brigade
Third (Crawford's) Division
Fifth (Sykes') Corps
Army of the Potomac
Mustered into Pennsylvania Service
June 8, 1861
Mustered into Federal Service
July 26, 1861
Mustered Out
June 13, 1864

The left reads:

> Recruited in Adams County, the men of Company K partici-
> pated in eight battles: Mechanicsville, Gaines Mill, Glendale,
> South Mountain, Gettysburg, Wilderness, Spotsylvania, and
> Bethesda Church. The casualties sustained were 17 who died in service and 23
> who were wounded.

The right reads:

> During the Battle of Gettysburg on July 2, 1863, the men of
> Company K, in the center of the First Reserves, helped to repulse
> the Confederate attempt to seize Little Round Top, possession of
> which was the key to victory in the battle.

The bottom center reads:

> This monument was erected in 1991 by the Adams County
> Company K Memorial Committee as a remembrance of the more
> than 2,000 Adams Countians who participated in the American
> Civil War, waged between 1861 and 1865 in a successful effort to
> preserve the Federal Union.

The monument to the 30th Infantry, 1st Pennsylvania Reserves, stands along Ayres Avenue on the eastern edge of the "Wheatfield." At the base of the shaft is the inscription: Co. K recruited at Gettysburg. The monument was dedicated in September, 1890.

INTRODUCTION

To lay joking aside, it was a serious matter to be summoned to the defense of our homes. We had gone out two years before, to conquer the enemy on his own soil, but were now returning, after two years of struggle, to meet him face to face at our own door. What the feeling of each member of the company was, under these circumstances, may be better imagined than described, for we had seen enough of the ravages of warfare in the south-land, to cause us to be anxious for the welfare of our loved ones, now exposed in like manner.

It was more than a quarter of a century after the Battle of Gettysburg that Henry Naleigh Minnigh, Captain of Company K, 1st Pennsylvania Reserves sat down at his desk to record for posterity a history of his unit in the great Civil War. Known as "the Boys who fought at home," Company K had the distinction of being one of a few companies in the Army of the Potomac recruited from Adams County, Pennsylvania, to fight at Gettysburg. In the summer of 1863, Company K suddenly found itself experiencing what tens of thousands of their Confederate counterparts had felt for the last two years—the compelling need to defend to the death their homes, their land, and their loved ones. No longer had the war become a struggle solely to preserve the Union. For the men of Company K, Robert E. Lee's invasion of Pennsylvania had aroused their worst fears, and with each mile closer to Gettysburg, their anxiety grew. Seldom in the history of the American Civil War do we find a company of Union soldiers that fought to defend the threshold of their very homes. Instead we are accustomed to reading of the valiant defense of home and hearth from the Confederate viewpoint, a defense that despite superhuman effort left the South a land of great devastation with cities ruined, land scorched, and economies destroyed. It is little wonder then, that Henry Minnigh would not hesitate to mention the feelings of his men on the eve of the greatest battle ever fought in the Western Hemisphere. For them Gettysburg was the pivotal point of the war. But Minnigh's account is more than just a history of Gettysburg. It is a compilation of the wartime experiences of the men who made up this famous "Gettysburg" unit. Although Minnigh wrote his history almost thirty years after the war, it was clearly designed to be a publication for his former comrades and their families rather than a unit history to be shared with the masses. Unlike the thick, weighty volumes written by other veterans, Minnigh's work is short and elementary, knowing full well that his readers experienced first hand the important events and incidents of the war. For him there was no need to belabor the causes of the war or the grand strategies and intricate maneuvers of great armies. Instead, Minnigh's humble account became a personal testimony to be shared among a "band of brothers" that comprised but a microcosm of the Army of the Potomac. In this approach, however, there are both strengths and weaknesses to *The History of Company K*. Absent are those little details that are found in larger regimentals, details that Civil War historians spend years looking for when studying the great campaigns and personalities. Sizeable gaps also appear throughout the narrative making the reader wonder what occurred between the great battles that Minnigh failed to mention. The details of the company during most battles are absent leaving one to ponder how well the unit performed in combat. As the Captain wrote in his preface:

> *We have sought to gather...a few of the incidents that are prominent in the History of Company K...after the facts have passed almost beyond recall. We have been obliged, for the sake of brevity, to omit much that might have been recorded, and to give only that, which we think should be preserved in some way.*

Unfortunately, by selecting his audience Minnigh knowingly or unknowingly left the rest of the world out of the great story that was "the history of Company K." One obvious strength of the work is how Minnigh organized his narrative. He divided the book into three sections: a brief history of the unit from 1861-1864, a muster roll of the company, and a selection of human interest stories throughout the war by its members. The muster roll is quite valuable in discussing the composition of the "boys who fought at home." Here the reader finds personal tidbits about the officers and men, their occupations and ages, service record and their loss in battle. But perhaps the most delightful section of the narrative is entitled "Reminiscences." Here one finds a compilation of recollections that makes Minnigh's work so worthwhile. In these pages are the likes of such wonderful characters as "Snap" Rouzer and Bill Mumper and incredibly funny as well as serious incidents of soldier life. Minnigh's own daring account of visiting his family in Gettysburg on July 3 is as wonderful in its drama as it is in its poignancy. Braving sharpshooters' bullets while dodging from alley to fence, he reached his home only to find his family hiding in the cellar out of harm's way. And when he finally speaks to his family after two years of absence they fail to recognize him as their own son. Only in these pages do we, nearly a century and a half later, begin to understand and appreciate the struggles and sacrifices of those men both blue and gray, who gave their lives "that this nation might live." Minnigh's story is balanced, told not only through the eyes of an officer who led the company in battle, but also from the perspective of the enlisted man. Minnigh himself enlisted as a member of the company only hours before its departure from Gettysburg for Philadelphia. During the summer of 1861 he drilled as a "high private in the rear rank" until being promoted to fourth sergeant in early September. He served in this capacity until the end of the Peninsular Campaign when battle losses caused his promotion to second lieutenant. Although badly wounded in the left arm at South Mountain, he returned to duty after a short convalescence, finally commanding the company as captain from Chancellorsville until being mustered out in June 1864. Henry Minnigh was obviously well-liked and respected by the members of Company K. He was described by many as kind-hearted, with a deep and abiding concern for the health, well-being and morale of his men, not just because they were his soldiers, but more importantly, because they were also his neighbors and friends before the war. Not every officer could claim such a tribute, and his sensitivity for others earned him much appeal in later life as a minister. His account of the death of Lt. J. Durbin Sadler at South Mountain and the determination to take his body home for proper burial is a wonderful example of Minnigh's devotion to his men. Facing arrest and potential execution as a deserter if discovered, Minnigh disguised himself as a civilian in order to escort his friend's body 54 miles through Maryland to Sadler's home in York Springs, Pennsylvania. As for bravery there is no doubt. Any man who charged down the northwestern slope of Little Round Top into the Plum Run valley and stemmed the tide of

Longstreet's attacks across the Wheatfield late on July 2 earned the title of "soldier." One comrade said that his record "is an enviable one. He led the company with gallantry and spirit on all occasions, securing the commendations of his superior officers, for bravery under trying circumstances." After reading this little volume one wishes that Minnigh had not been so selfish in his desire to "omit much that might have been recorded" and to give only that "which we think should be preserved in some way." By compiling these recollections only for those who shared the experience, many generations to come were denied the opportunity to learn from those experiences, and to understand why one man, a group of men, or an entire nation, would sacrifice everything for their beliefs. Sadly, like many other units who served in the Civil War, so little was left behind by "the Boys who fought at home." Nevertheless, we should cherish what memories have been passed down to us, especially those that flowed from the pen of Henry Minnigh.

Paul M. Shevchuk
Gettysburg, Pennsylvania
September 6, 1996

CONTENTS

HISTORY
OF

COMPANY K.

1st (Inft,) Penn'a Reserves.

"𝕮𝖍𝖊 𝕭𝖔𝖞𝖘 𝖜𝖍𝖔 𝖋𝖔𝖚𝖌𝖍𝖙 𝖆𝖙 𝕳𝖔𝖒𝖊,"

BY H. N. MINNIGH.
Captain and Brev. Major.

Introductory Edition.

"Home Print" Publisher.
DUNCANSVILLE., PA.

TO

WIVES,
DAUGHTERS,
FATHERS & MOTHERS,
WHO GAVE THEIR LOVED ONES
TO THE UNION CAUSE,
THIS LITTLE VOLUME IS
RESPECTFULLY
DEDICATED,

BY

THE AUTHOR.

AUTHOR'S PREFACE.

WE have sought to gather into this little volume, a few of the incidents that are prominent in the History of Company K, as they have presented them-selves to us, after the facts related have passed almost beyond recall. We have been obliged, for the sake of brevity, to omit much that might have been recorded, and to give only that, which we think should be pre-served in some way.

Our Children, and Children's children, as they scan these pages in the days to come, may proudly boast of ancestors, who were among "The Boys who fought at Gettysburg their own home."

We are aware that inaccuracies and imperfections will be found in the book. for while the collecting of material has been in progress for quite a while, the edi-ting and compiling, has come upon us in the midst of other cares and duties, in our chosen walk of life.

Preface.

We trust our labor will not be in vain, but that our little volume will be appreciated and preserved, by those still in life, who remember the scene and experience so imperfectly set forth, as well as by their pasterity, through all time to come.

We have already commenced the revision of this volume, and propose soon to publish a larger and revised edition; and, therefore, I ask all comrades who may find errors in the present edition, to acquaint me at once of the fact, that such errors may be corrected.

H. N. M.

TRANSCRIPT
of the
MUSTER OUT ROLL
Of Co. K. First Penn'a Reserves.

WE give only a Transcript of names, as they appear on the Muster Out Roll, referring our readers to the Historical Record, for the date of Muster in and Muster out, and all other interesting data. This Roster includes the names of all the members of the company, that ever appeared on any muster roll.

❋ MUSTER OUT ROLL. ❋

Present.

1. Henry N. Minnigh,   Captain.
2. George E. Kitzmiller, 1st Lieut.

1. Samuel A. Young, 1st Sergeant
2. John C. Brandon,   Sergeant.
3. James McGonigle,   do
4. M. Murray Miller,   do

1. Henry H. Beamer,   Corporal.
2. James Culbertson,   do
3. George C. Carson,   do
4. John F. Mackley,   do
5. Andrew A. Slagle,   do

Muster Out Roll.

1. Beales Charles W,   Private.
2. Bingaman Samuel,   do
3 Blocher Andrew H,   do
4. Caufman Henry W,   do
5. Cox George W,   do
6. Danner H. Knox,   do
7. Dixon Samuel,   do
8. Gibbs George W,   do
9. Jacobs John H. K,   do
10. Johns David E,   do
11. Jobe William T,   do
12. Mackley Jacob,   do
13. Megary William R,   do
14. Robison D. Webster,   do
15. Rouzer James M,   do
16. Riggs William,   do
17. Remmel David E. H,   do
18. Stewart David M,   do
19. Stouffer Jacob,   do

Discharged.

1. Edward McPherson,   Captain.
2. J. J. Herron,   1st Lieut.

[Discharged, continued.]

1. Philip L. Houck,   Sergeant.
2. Peter H. Henry,   do
3. Alex. L. C. Woods,   do

1 Charles Z. Tawney,   Corporal.

1. Caufman Charles E,   Private.
2. Eyster Samuel H,   do
3. Devine Bernard,   do
4. Dixon Samuel,   do
5. Fanus Hiram J,   do
6. Hart Levi J,   do
7. Hollinger Philip,   do
8. Hortkins Henry,   do
9. Lady Hiram,   do
10. Myers John J,   do
11. Pierce James Shaw,   do
12. Rhoads Andrew H,   do
13. Shaffer David,   do
14. Siplinger Mathias J,   do
15. Trimmer William,   do

Muster Out Roll.

Transferred.

1.	W. W. Stewart,	Captain.
1.	Peter S. Harbaugh,	Sergeant.
1.	Joseph Hamilton,	Corporal.
2.	Joseph Baker,	do
3.	Robert T. McKinney,	do
4.	Jacob Resser,	do
5.	Daniel D. Bailey,	do
6.	Brandon Isaac M,	do
1.	Gilbert Charles E,	Musician.
2.	Naylor Wilson E,	do
1.	Arendt Jacob W,	Private.
2.	Beard Obed. M,	do
3.	Chronister Amos,	do
4.	Cassatt Samuel J,	do
5.	Duey John J,	do
6.	Durboraw I. Newton,	do
7.	Elden Henry W. C,	do
8.	Gardner Amos T,	do
9.	Goutermuth Paul,	do
10.	Hamilton Calvin,	do
11.	Harbaugh Calvin,	do

Transferred, [continued.]

12.	Keckler Samuel E,	Private.
13.	Leech Elijah L,	do
14.	Monteer Henry R,	do
15.	Mumper William,	do
16.	Myers David M,	do
17.	Pittinger John F,	do
18.	Pensyl George W,	do
19.	Rosensteel John H,	do
20.	Sheads Robert E,	do
21.	Sheets Samuel,	do
22.	Swisher Charles E,	do
23.	Woodring David H,	do
24.	Foutz Adam	do
25.	Ogden John Q,	do

Died.

1.	Bailey J. Findley,	Captain.
2.	Sadler John D,	1st Lieut.
1.	Creamer John T,	Private.
2.	Keim Frederick A,	do
3.	McKinney John W,	do
4.	Miller Peter M,	do

5.	McGrew William,	Private.
6.	Myers George W,	do
7.	Nailor Jeremiah,	do
8.	Shank Jesse,	do
9.	Shipley John W,	do
10.	Wisotzkey Craig F,	do

Deserters.

1.	Bingaman David,	Private.
2.	Gardner Richard P,	do
3.	Hart Bernard,	do
4.	Hildebrand John F,	do
5.	Jones Henry H,	do
6.	Metcalf Wooster B,	do
7.	Weber Frank,	do

Dropped.

1.	Gibson John,	Private.
2.	Holtzworth Adam,	do
3.	Holtzworth George,	do
4.	Little George,	do
5.	Rogers Zephaniah,	do
6.	Zell William,	do

A HISTORY
OF COMPANY K. FIRST (Inft.) PENN'A RESERVES.

INTRODUCTORY.

IS our purpose, to write a brief History of Company K. First (Inft,) Penn'a Reserves.

The history of a Company, as duty was performed by such command, in the War of the Rebellion, must needs be, the History of the Regiment, Brigade and Division to which such company belonged.

It is not a part of our plan, to add laurels to those really won by the company, or to burnish the charac- of any member thereof, for the record is already made, and this Company needs no boosting into popular favor at this late day.

That the History of the company and of its heroes, may be put into tangible form for distribution and preservation, as well as that a book of reference may be put in the hands of the survivors and their families, is our only object.

Company K. First Penn'a Reserves, takes no second place among the companies that went out from the County of Adams, though other companies performed good and noble service.

I wish to confine myself mainly, to Three points of interest, in the work assumed :

I. The Organization and work of the Company.

II. A brief Record of each member.

III. Reminiscences of the Company.

CHAPTER I.

Organization of the Company.

ON THE 15th day of May, 1861, a Bill was passed by both branches of the Penn'a Legislature, received the Governor's signature, and became a law of the commonwealth, authorizing the organization of a military corps, to be called, the Reserve volunteer corps, to be composed of Thirteen regiments of Infantry, One of Cavalry and One of Artillery, to be mustered into the State service, and to be liable to be mustered into the service of the United States at any time. (See Bill.)

In response to orders issued to local military organizations in the state, the "Adams county infantry," of Gettysburg, accepted the call. The ranks were filled to the maximum number, in a few days, from all parts of the county, and was officered as follows :—

Edward McPherson, Captain; J. Finley Bailey, 1st Lieut ; J. J. Herron, 2nd Lieut.

We rendezvoused at Gettysburg on Friday June 7.
1861, having been accepted by Gov. Curtin, under the
provisions of the Bill above recorded.

On Saturday June 8th, at 7:30 a. m. the command
took the train, and proceeded to Camp Wayne, at
Westchester, Pa., where a Camp was organized under
charge of Capt. H. M. McIntire, as a rendezvous, for
a portion of the Reserve corps.

We reached Camp at 6:30 p. m. and entered upon
an experience, which few suspected would last for the
whole term of three years.

CHAPTER II.

Organization was effected, by the
appointment of non-Commissioned officers, on Tuesday June 11th
as follows:—

W. W. Stewart, 1st Sergeant, and
J. J. Duey, Peter H. Henry. and
H. N. Minnigh, Sergeants, in the
order named ; also, the following Corporals :— J. D.
Sadler, P. L. Houck, Jacob Resser and D. D. Bailey.

The Record will prove whether these were judicious
selections or not.

"After muster into the State service, our progress in the drill was so marked, that Col. Roberts, on account of the character of the men and their proficiency, selected us as Company B, of the Regiment," says Capt. McPherson in a recent letter, "an assignment which was overruled by Gen'l McCall, when the regiment reached Washington. The Union guards of Lancaster, which had originally been Co. B, was thereby restored and we were made, as at first, Co. K, which position had naturally fallen to us, having been the last company of those forming the First regiment, that arrived in camp."

Well! we have the consciousness today, that as a company we were not inferior to any other command in the regiment, and Company K. never did and never will, ask for unmerited favors.

On June 18, a slashing and cutting affray took place in camp, for on that day a general vaccination of the members of the company was ordered. Probably the Surgeon wanted to get a little practice. He got there.

June 20, the ladies of our native county, sent us a full complement of Havelocks, and a useless appendage they were. Barney D. said, they were "Moighty noice to corrie me tobaccy in." We sent home thanks and threw the "head-bags" away.

Drill, drill, drill! was the order of the camp, and we soon became proficient in all company movements, principally under the command of Lieut. Bailey.

Col. Roberts took command of the Regiment, and also of the camp, on June 20th, and on the 21st, Capt. McPherson visited Gettysburg, returning on the 25th, bringing five recruits for the company, which added to the 69 who had passed the examination previously, increased our numer to 74.

June 28th, we again received a donation from home, consisting of needle-cases, which were very convenient, but one of the boys said, he wished his sister, or somebody else's sister, had come along to do his mending.

On Monday, July 1st, the regiment was partly uniformed ; white duck pants and flannel shirts, furnished by the state, and a fancy gray Jacket, sent from home, while Caps and Overcoats, were issued by the government; arms and accoutrements, were also distributed.

"The Glorious Fourth," came on, and with it came an invitation to a neighboring grove, where the good people of Westchester furnished us with a No. 1. dinner. After dinner the "shoulder straps" gallanted the girls, while the "low private" soldiers looked on, or perhaps thought of "The girl I left behind me." Some took a bathe in the Brandywine.

July 5th, an order was issued, requiring all companies to be filled up to the maximum number, by recruiting officers, sent out for that purpose. It should have
been stated before, that at the original examination, a
nnmber of men had been rejected, on account of physical defects, even the slightest, as only men of perfect
physique were taken to fill the quota.

Sergeants Stewart and Minnigh were detailed accordingly, leaving camp on the 8th, and returning on the
19th, with twenty recruits, who were mustered in on
that date, increasing our numbers to 94 all told.

While we still lacked seven of the full quota, the
very best material, however, composed this command,
men of muscle, nerve, and courage, as well as brain,
men of whom Gov. Curtin could well say, "They are
the flower of the state." All volunteers, none forced
into service, no bummers, no bounty-jumpers.

Another fact should be stated here; the men in the
ranks were not inferior, in physique or social standing
to the officers. Hence, the duty performed, and the
work done by this command.

Every battle-field on which the Army of the Potomac was engaged, from Mechanicsville, June 26. 1862,
to Bethesda church, June 30. 1864, drank of the noblest blood, the state could afford, when these men fell.

CHAPTER III.

"On To The Front."

CAMP Wayne was left behind, on July 21st, when the First regiment with other Reserve troops, were ordered to rendezvous at Harrisburg, on their way to the front.

All along the way, from the latter place, the people were in the rage of excitement, owing to the disaster at Bull-run, the previous day, (21st,) and when we reached Baltimore, a delegation of the city authorities and police, waited on Col. Roberts, who was in command of all troops then moving to the front, and urged him not to attempt a passage through the city. Our commanders characteristic reply was, "Gentlemen! we have not come down here hunting for safe places, my men are thoroughly equipped, and will march through the city."

On the morning of the 23rd, we advanced through the city, the only peculiarity, noticeable, being the scarcity of Baltimore fire-eaters and plug-uglies.

Having passed through the heart of the city without any disturbance whatever, we camped on Carroll Hill, in the suburbs, and here on the 24th of July, we were mustered into the U. S. Service, for three years or during the war.

July 26th, the non-Commissioned officers were increased to 5 sergeants, and 8 corporals, A. L. C. Woods being appointed 5th sergeant, and S. A. Young, I. N. Durboraw, I. M. Brandon and H. W. Caufman, 5th; 6th, 7th an l 8th corporals, respectively.

On the 28th, we left this camp, and marched toward Washington D. C. but at Annapolis Junction we, with three other companies of the regiment, went into camp, while the ballance of the regiment went to Annapolis.

Lieut. Herron resigned on the 14th, and Capt. Mc Pherson on the 24th of August; an election was accordingly held, and resulted in the promotion of W. W, Stewart, to 1st Lieut. and J. D. Sadler, to 2nd Lieut. while Lieut. Bailey was made Captain in the regular line of promotion.

On August 30th, we moved with the regiment, to camp Tennally, north west of Wasington city, and at no great distance from the same.

Here a general promotion of non-commissioned officers took place, and when finished, they stood in the following order on the company rolls.

H. N. Minnigh, Orderly Serg't, J. J. Duey, P. H.
Henry, A. L. C. Woods and P. L. Houck, Sergeants
in the order named.   S. A. Young, I. N. Durboraw,
I. M. Brandon, H. W. Caufman, C. Z. Tawney, Geo.
E. Kitzmiller, H. Knox Danner and Jacob Resser,
Corporals.

Eight recruits joined the company and were mustered
in Sep't 3rd, beside these, only six others ever joined
the company, and they came and were mustered in on
Sep't 4th, 1862. (See roll.)

September 16th, the Penn'a Reserves, were fully organized as a Division, with Gen'l Geo. A. McCall as
Division commander, and Gen'l Jno. F. Reynolds, in
command of the First Brigade, to which Brigade our
Regiment was attached.

And now followed many weary days, consisting of
Company, Regimental and Brigade drill, also, daily
details of men, who assisted in building Fort Pennsylvania, erected by the Reserves, an occasional review
or "F A L L I N," which merely meant an exhaustive
standing in line for hours together, "the divil knows
phwat fore," said Barney, none of which was much
enjoyed by the boys, who were eager to cross the Potomac, whip the Jonnies, and then go home. Many
amusing things transpired at this camp, of which we
may speak later on.

CHAPTER IV.

The Work of the Company.

WITH Chapter Fourth, we enter upon the Second division of our projected plan, viz., "The work of the company."

October 9th, we crossed the Potomac river, and entered upon the "sacred soil of Virginia," and formed a winter camp at Langley, known as Camp Pierpont.

Here we tried to be comfortable, but the severe exposure with constant camp and picket duty, wrought upon the men who never knew else, than to live under the sheltering roofs of comfortable homes, "up in the north-land."

November 26. Jesse Shank, of York Springs, Pa, and December 4, Geo. W. Myers, of the same place, died, and were sent home for burial. But the winter wore away, and weary of the monotonous routine of duty, we waited eagerly for the spring-time, and the anticipated forward movement.

March 10, we broke camp and joined in the advance of the Army of the Potomac, under Gen'l G .B. McClellan, and on the evening of the first days march, camped at Hunter's Mill, Va.

We stayed here three days, and then moved in the direction of Alexandria, where we arrived, through rain and mud, and went into camp, the advance movement having developed the fact, that the confederate army had abandoned Manasses and gone southward.

April 9th, we moved forward on the line of the Orange & Alex'a R. R. by way of Manasses and Warrenton junctions, to Catlett's station, and finally down the north bank of the Rappahannock river to Falmouth opposite Fredericksburg, where we encamped.

May 26th, we crossed the river, and took possession of that city, encamping on the heights westward.

This, and the former camp at Falmouth, were decidedly the pleasantest camps in our three years service.

On June 8th, the Division was ordered to join McClellan's forces on the peninsula. We accordingly embarked at Bell's landing on the 9th, and after a voyage of 20 hours, disembarked at White-house landing on the Pamunkey river. After various marches and counter-marches we finally encamped on June 18th, on the extreme right of the army, near Mechanicsville.

And now came the famous Seven days Battles, the very thought of which, causes an involuntary tremor to pass through the whole being, days of horror and bloodshed, of humiliation and death. We cannot even hope to give an adequate portrayal of these horrors.

CHAPTER V.

Battle of Mechanicsville.

THE 26th of June, found the command on the Picket line, from which we were hurriedly recalled, only to find our camp had disappeared and our private property gone "where the woodbine twineth," but in time to take our place in line with other troops, who were ready to meet the confederates, who were reported as advancing in our immediate front. We were ordered by special detail with our Regiment, to support Cooper's battery. I need not write up this battle in full detail, for those *who were there*, remember well, the onward rush of the enemy, how two whole divisions under Gen'l Lee, (a fact developed more recently,) at 3 p. m. threw themselves upon our line, only to be hurled back amid great slaughter, how amid the shriek of shell and flashing musketry they still advanced, how our 69 caliber elongated balls now for the first time were sent on missions of death, and with what execution, how Craig Wisotskey fell, and in few moments expired, one limb being literally torn from the body, when Hamilton and Siplinger were wounded and assisted from the field, how at length the the shades of night fell, putting an end to the conflict.

There was no movement of troops in the Union lines, the men stood in their places and poured an uninterrupted fire upon the enemy, while the artillery, fifty pieces, rained solid shot, shells, canister and sharpnell, producing great slaughter. The total Union loss in this battle was eighty killed and two hundred wounded, while the Rebel loss was three thousand.

We slept on our arms that night, and at the early dawn we were withdrawn, contrary to the wishes of the Reserves who had held the ground against five times their number, but we did not then know that Jackson had come from the Shenandoah with 40,000 men, and was in our rear.

The forces north of the Chickahominy took up a new position at Gaines' mill, sometimes called Gaines' hill, and by the rebels, Coal Harbor. Gen'l Porter is in command with 40,000 men while Gen'l Lee is coming on with 70,000, he intends to make a grand onset and sweep Porter into the Chickahominy. Three o'clock of the 27th, has come and the attack is made, amid cannonry and the angry flashes of musketry, while the battle cloud becomes thick and heavy. It would take many pages to make a full record of the terrible battle.

At 4 o'clock we were ordered to the support of the Duryea Zouaves, which regiment had been almost annihilated. We checked the enemy and held the line

until every cartridge is gone, when we were relieved.
Just behind the front line we halted, when a charge by
the enemy broke the Union line, and a mass of disorganized troops came rushing back. It was at this juncture Gen'l Porter said, "Col. Roberts, can't you form
a line and stop those flying troops?" to which our
brave Colonel responded, "I can Gen'l, but send me
ammunition to stop the enemy." Steadily as if on dress
parade, the regiment faced fleeing friends, halted the
disorganized mass, rallied them under its colors, and
then with fixed bayonet awaited the onset. But cheers
are heard coming from our rear, the tramp of some
body of troops hurrying forward, and the famous Irish
Brigade push onward with long and steady step, they
check the enemy and drive him back, the day is won,
and quiet is restored again.

We crossed to the south side of the Chickahominy
during the night, and joined the general retreat toward the James river, the Division having charge of all
the ammunition and other trains. This consumed our
time till the evening of the 29th, when the command
is sent out on the road leading from Charles' city to
Richmond, west of our line of retreat, this being the
most dangerous line of approach from the confederate
side. All remember that terrible night while on picket duty, for it was soon discovered that a large force

of the enemy were quietly concentrating in our front. At day light we fell back to the line of battle composed of the division of Penn'a Reserves, who were in advance of all other troops, and awaited the onset.

Half-past two o'clock came, and then Hill with six brigades of his own and six of Longstreets command, hurled the whole force upon our front. Brigade after brigade advanced, but recoiled under the direct fire of the batteries, sustained by the infantry.

"Volley after volley streamed across our front and in such quick succession that it seemed impossible for any human being to live under it," writes a Rebel officer. "Use the bayonet only," is our standing order, as counter-charges are directed against the enemy, and thus for three hours the battle rages, sustained wholly by McCall's division of less than six thousand men, and Hill has not driven him an inch.

It was then that J. Finley Bailey our brave Captain was last seen, and strange as it may seem, no has ever been found who knew aught of his fate. Lieut. Stewart was wounded while acting adjutant of the regiment, while nine men were wounded and eight taken prisoner. The Irish brigade again came to the rescue, at about sunset, and under cover of the night, we fell back to the James river at Malvern Hill, in a state of complete exhaustion and despondency.

At the battle of Malvern hill, our command took no active part, but were held in reserve, the only time in our recollection that we held such a position.

It may be said here, and the statistics proves the fact, that the Penn'a Reserves sustained a loss during the seven days battles, of one-fifth of the total loss, while our strength was only one-fifteenth of the total strength, and this fact does not find a parallel, in any campaign or any battle, of any division of the federal army, east or west.

CHAPTER VI.

At Harrison's Landing.

BUT the campaign is ended, and on July 3rd, we go into camp at Harrison's landing, six miles down the James river.

Here we suffer many hardships on account of inferior rations and unwholesome water, producing malarious and chronic diseases, and this we endured for forty-two days.

A regular promotion of company officers took place here, as follows :— W. W. Stewart to be Captain, J. D. Sadler, 1st Lieut. and H. N. Minnigh, 2nd Lieut. Sadler was in command Stewart being absent wounded.

August the 15th, we took the lead in the evacuation
of the Peninsula, and embarked on the steamer Rob't
Morrison, for the avowed purpose of joining Pope's
army before Washington. We landed at Aquia creek,
on the 19th, and proceeding thence by way of Fredericksburg, and at Warrenton junction, we fell in with
Pope's forces, hurrying back toward the National capitol, with the rebel horde at his heels.

We reached Bull Run on the 29th, and found that
a portion of the rebel army had beat us in the race,
but by a flank movement we passed them, took up a
position on the old battle ground, skirmished back and
forth one whole day, and waited eagerly the coming
of McClellan's army.

After a brave and obstinate contest, lasting all day
on the 30th, in which a victory should have been won,
but was lost through the defection and petty jealousies
of some leading officers, the Union forces yielded the
ground and fell back toward Washington.

On the night of Sep't 1st, we picketed on the flank
of the army camped at Centreville, then joined in the
general retreat and finally went into camp at Upton's
hill, near Alexandria.

September 6th, we moved across the Long Bridge,
through Washington city, to Leesboro, Md. where we
went into camp.

The Rebel army under Gen'l Lee, has crossed the Potomac near Point of Rocks, and it is his intention to "liberate Maryland, and invade Pennsylvania."

His plan is to hold the gaps across South Mountain, and push his army north through the rich and beautiful Cumberland valley, "cut his way to Philadelphia, and dictate terms of peace in Independence Square."

On September 14th, the Union army found the enemy well posted on the mountain twelve miles west of Frederick city, and four miles from Middletown, and the Union veterans of the Peninsula, hurried up to meet him. Reaching the foot of the mountain after a hurried march, we file to the right, then face to the front, and begin the ascent of the mountain. Onward, upward we sweep, like a great tidal wave, the foot of the last acclivity is reached, then with a cheer, we cross the stone wall in our front, and with a rush up through the corn field, then a short, desperate, decisive struggle, and the battle of South Mountain is won.

Lieut. J. D. Sadler in command of the company fell while gallantly leading his men in this charge, and at the same moment Jere. Naylor and Peter Miller, were killed, while Lieut. H. N. Minnigh and several men were wounded, leaving the company without a commissioned officer, Capt. Stewart still being absent, on account of wounds.

On September 17th, the command was at Antietam, and took its place in line, though the company only numbered ten or twelve men for duty, and were led by Serg't Kitzmiller, and fortunately no crsualties occurred, during that terrible struggle.

CHAPTER VII.

Forward once more.

THE COMPANY has now been in active service one year, and the ranks are reduccd from 94 to a mere guard of 30 present for duty, not one-third of the number is left, while the Penn'a Reserves, by the fatalities of warfare are reduced from the original 15,000 to barely 4,000 for duty.

The command went into camp near Sharpsburg, where 2nd Lieut. Minnigh was promoted to 1st Lieut. and Serg't Kitzmiller to 2nd Lieut. and Capt. Stewart returned to the company from Gen'l Hospital.

Breaking camp once more on October 30th, we recrossed the Potomac at Berlin ferry, going southward, through Lovettsville, Warrenton, Rappahannock station, and finally go into camp at Fredericksburg.

While here, and before the Fredericksburg campaign opened, Co. K, was detailed on special duty at Brooks' station, on the Aquia creek rail-road, and as a consequence did not participate in the Battle of the 10th of December, in which the Penn'a Reserves once more distinguished themselves, making a charge, that for dash and daring, has not a parallel in the entire history of the war. Of this charge a distinguished writer says, "They broke through two well entrenched lines of the enemy, and accomplished what was expected of them, but for want of support they were compeled to retire." The loss in this assault was 176 killed, 1197 wounded and 468 missing, a total loss of 1841, out of a possible 4500, two-fifths of the total loss reported in said battle. The detail of the company with the ambulance corps, did duty on the field.

On February 8th, the whole command was relieved from the front, and transferred to the defences of the city of Washington, to afford an opportunity, it was said, to recruit our decimated ranks and wasted energies, but as the event proved, in the 1st Regiment at least, to perform more arduous duty than we had done when with the main army. Our camp was located on the north bank of the historic Bull-run, and finally at Fairfax court-house. It was here the famous Photo of company K. was taken, June 4th, 1863.

The battle of Chancellorsville, was fought on May 2nd, and when the Army of the Potomac followed on the flank of Lee's forces which were moving northward, we rejoined our old comrades, in pursuit of the enemy.

CHAPTER VIII.

GETTYSBURG.

HAVING crossed the Potomac at Edward's ferry a continuous march on June 28, 29, 30 and July 1, and 2, brought us to Gettysburg our own native town, and HOME. Before reaching Gettysburg we heard various rumors of the investment of our home by the enemy. One incident may be related here; When approaching the familliar haunts of former days, and some of the company began to recogize well known faces, though themselves unknown, it was amusing to note the surprise' of the citizens, upon hearing their names deliberately called out by the unknown soldiers. One aged citizen when convined of identity of his own nephew, said "Vy Chon, for vat de defil you left dem repel soljers gum up heyr, Hey?" John's reply was, "Why! Uncle Sam, it was all planned out so that I could get home to see my Mammy."

To lay joking aside, it was a serious matter to be

thus summoned in defence of our own homes. We had gone out two years before, to conquer the enemy on his own soil, but were now returning, after two years of struggle, to meet him face to face at our own door. What the feeling of each member of the company was, under these circumstances, may be better imagined than described, for we had seen enough of the ravages of warfare in the south-land, to cause us to be anxious for the welfare of our loved ones, now exposed in like manner.

As we neared Gettysburg, in a number of instances we passed near the homes of relatives and friends, but with the merest greeting, the boys kept their places in the ranks. Reaching the summit of the hill east of the town, the members of the company, with a few exceptions, could see their homes, in the village before them, in the immediate vicinity or in the distance, and all of them within the enemy's lines.

We reached Gettysburg on the morning of July 2nd, coming from the direction of Hanover, and moving to the left went into bivouac near the Baltimore pike, one mile east of Cemetery ridge. Fatigued by the long and weary marches, we soon were oblivious to all surroundings, wrapped in restful slumber, unbroken even by the terrible fighting at Culp's hill and Cemetery ridge, on our immediate right and front.

About 4 o'clock we were hurriedly called into line,
and ordered to sling knapsacks, which command to us
always meant, "get ready for quick and devilish work,"
as "Snap" put it. We were hurried at a double quick
to the exteeme left, at the Round tops, to re-inforce
the 3rd Corps, which had met with reverses and was
being driven by the enemy. Gen. Sykes' Regulars had
previously gone to the support of Sickles, but had also
yielded the ground. A terrible crisis was now seemingly inevitable. The Regulars were the last to yield the
ground, but being flanked on their left, they broke
and fell back in disorder. At this juncture, we came
upon the ground. The First Brigade, formed hurriedly in brigade front, as best they could, the nature of
the ground compelling the regiments to overlap each
other to some extent, on the crest of Little Round top,
facing the Wheat field. As we thus formed, we looked
down over the field of carnage, and could hear the
victorious shouts of the enemy, and when the smoke
of battle lifted momentarily, we caught glimpses of
fleeing friends and hotly pursuing foes, the general
outlook being anything but assuring.

We deliberately waited till the front was cleared of
our retreating and vanquished troops, many of whom
passed pell-mell through our ranks, then at the word
of command, with a ringing cheer, peculiarly our own,

we swept down the face of the hill, meeting the rebels
as they came rushing forward, on the face of the hill,
(I can only speak for my own regiment.) There can
be no doubt in any unprejudiced mind, that a few moments delay would have lost to us the position on
Little Round Top, the key of the battle-field. The so
called historian of the battle-field, asserts that there
were no rebels in our front when we charged forward.
Nonesense! the evidence of those who were there, we
think, should have more weight than that of a mere
citizen hundreds of miles away from the field of strife.
Well, with a quick dash we swept down into the valley,
across Plum-run swamp, over the valley and up to the
stone fence, across this fence and through a narrow
strip of woods, (now removed,) to the eastern edge of
the wheat-field, where, by orders, we halted.

It has always been a source of amusement to the
"boys" who chased many a rabbit all over these hills,
and gathered berries in these valleys, played "hide
and seek" among these rocks and boulders, to be told
by strangers and pretenders, where we were, on the
evening of July 2nd, when the enemy had almost seiz-
ed this strong-hold, at the Round Tops.

The comrades will remember the commander of the
battery in our immediate front, who raved and swore,
when it seemed as if his guns would be taken.

"Dunder and blixen, don't let dem repels took my batteries," were his earnest words of appeal, as the enemy hurried up to the position occupied by his battery, and how, the next morning he came over to the stone wall and said, "The Pennsylvania Reserves saved mine pattery, by ——. I gets you fellers all drunk mit beer."

During the night of the 2nd, and all day of the 3rd till Pickets' charge ended, we remained at the stone wall, being compelled all the while to "lay low" on account of rebel sharp-shooters in our immediate front.

Pickets charge having failed, Gen. Meade ordered Crawford to clean out the woods in our front, and Mc Candles's (our) brigade at the word of command, leaped over the wall and deliberately dressed their lines. Skirmishers were deployed to the front, right and left, and the charge was made diagonally over the wheatfield to the southwest, to the woods on the west side, then half-wheeled to the right, then on up through the woods to the crest of the hill, driving the enemy out of the woods in the direction cf the Peach-orchard. The rebels at this juncture threatening our left flank, the column changed direction by left flank to the rear, and in this new direction we charged forward again. Down through the low land, then up through the woods east of the Rose house, surprising and capturing many prisoners, over three thousand muskets, and the colors of the Fifteenth Georgia regiment.

We bivouaced at night in the edge of Rose's woods, and abont noon being relieved, we moved back to the stone wall, and then to the rear of Little Round Top, where we went into bivouac, the battle being ended.

A few of the boys of Co. K, now went home, with or without leave, and who will blame them, each one returning in time to join in pursuit of the rebel horde as they fled southward from Gettysburg.

CHAPTER IX.

In pursuit of the rebels.

WE FOLLOWED the enemy closely in his retreat, keeping on his flank, and on July 11th, found him entrenched at Williamsport, Md. on the Potomac River.

On the 14th, when an advance was ordered upon these works, they were found abandoned, the enemy having re-crossed the river on the night of the 13th.

We followed on in due time, and soon found ourselves once more, back on the old line of the Rappahannock in Virginia, where after a most wearisome campaign, we went into camp.

About the middle of October, the enemy made an attempt to get between the federal forces and Washington city, but Gen. Meade defeated his purposes, and Lee went back to his old haunts beyond the Rapidan river.

November 6th, the Mine-run campaign opened, but beside constant skirmishing and several brisk battles, by portions of the army, nothing of importance was accomplished, and we returned to our old position on December 2nd.

During the balance of the winter of '63, '64, we were encamped at Bristow station, on the Orange and Alexandria Rail-road, and guarded well a portion of the line of communication.

CHAPTER X.

The Wilderness campaign.

APRIL 29th, we pulled up stakes again, and entered upon our last campaign. We broke camp and marched to Warrenton, a distance of thirty miles, and on the next morning continued on in the direction of Culpepper, and rejoined our old comrades of the main army, in the evening of that day.

We all knew that we were on the eve of an important campaign, and one that would in all probability close the war. The soldiers were very enthusiastic, and had the utmost confidence in the two great commanders who were to lead them.

On the 3rd of May there was great excitement in camp, and all anxiously waited for orders to move. The army had been reinforced, and everything now appeared to be in readiness to commence the campaign that was to end the war.

Directly after midnight, May 4th, the reveille was beat, and was heard echoing and re-echoing all along the line of camps, and soon after the great movement against the rebel capitol had begun. Our corps (the Fifth) moved in the direction of Germania ford on the Rapidan river, and having crossed at that point, we marched until four o'clock in the afternoon, when we halted for the night, having marched fully thirty miles. Our camp for the night was in the vicinity of the Wilderness tavern. About sunrise on the 5th we continued the march but had not gone far, when we found the enemy in our front. Preparation was immediately made to give them battle. Our position was on the Lacy farm, until ten o'clock, when we moved to Parker's store and formed line of battle, our regiment and the Bucktails being on the extreme left.

John W. Urban in his "Battle field and Prison pen"
says, "Capt. Wasson of Co. D, was ordered to take
his company and move through the woods beyond for
the purpose of reconnoitering the enemy's lines." This
is an error. The party was made up of a special detail
of twenty men, two from each company in the regiment. Captains Minnigh and Wasson were in charge,
and the actual mission was entirely unknown to Capt.
Wasson, who was ordered to take charge of the men
and assist Capt. Minnigh, in the duty which had been
secretly communicated to him. Wasson, nor any of the
men knew what was to be done. Fortunately, I have
in my possession the order, delivered to me, at Division Head-quarters, on said occasion. This order reads
as follows:—

"Captain, You will proceed, at once, to the front
bearing slightly to the left, to the Plank-road, and
(if possible,) find out what troops are moving on it &
in which direction they are moving."
It was intimated at the same time, that the mission
was of a *peculiar* character, and that Capt. Wasson,
would obey my orders.

Comrade Urban's description of our advance, is in
the main correct, but when we found the enemy before
us, I asked Capt. Wasson to withdraw a few paces into
the woods through which we had advanced, then and

there informing him of the orders placed in my hands.
He began at once to put on airs, (a habit of his,) and
positively refused to obey my orders. He advanced
the detail out into an open field, when one single shot
stampeded the party, and they returned to our line,
with the enemy on their heels.

I abandoned the detail hastily, and moving toward
the left parallel with the Plank-road, soon discovered
the enemy on that road, moving toward the extreme
right of the position occupied by the Union army,
which movement culminated in the attack on the out-
post position occupied by the Penn'a reserves, and
upon the Sixth corps later on.

Having accomplished my mission, I had no trouble
in getting back to our line, and reported to Head-
quarters, when the advance at the Parker house had
been forced back to the main line, and when the Seventh Reserves had been captured. My impression has
always been, that if Capt. Wasson had heeded my ad-
vice, the enemy would not have made the advance on
our front at Parker's, and the Seventh regiment would
not have been taken prisoners. I do not fear to speak
upon this point, as the question has been considerably
agitated, as to what led to the capture referred to.

If Co. D, was sent out on a reconnisance, as stated
by Urban, I am unacquainted with the fact.

Urban also says, that subsequently, "Lieut. Wilder, (we presume he means Weidler,) and ten men were sent on a reconnoisance in the same direction, and encountered the enemy, and after being driven back, Companies C and K were sent to dislodge them; but finding the enemy in strong force, fell back in haste to our lines."

It is not our object to contradict this last quotation, but it does seem to us, that this jumble of details from one single regiment, out of a whole division, needs an explanation at least.

A single proof of the correctness of the statement I have here made, is this:— Gen'l Crawford was much surprised when I reported to him, all begrimmed with dirt and smoke, having passed through the burning woods on my return to our line. Having reported, he said, "We never expected to see you again, ... but, your service shall be duly reported to the Secretary of war." This may account for the peculiar wording of the Commission as Brevet-Major, now in my possession, which reads as follows:— *"for gallant and meritorious services in the Wilderness campaign, Virginia, May 5,. 1864."* Here we leave this subject.

Safely back to the Lacy farm we rested for the night, waiting anxiously for the dawning of another day, that the terrible conflict might be continued.

Early on the morning of the 6th, the rebel forces were concentrated against Hancock on the left, where a terrible battle raged nearly all day. Such a continuous roar of musketry, inasmuch as artillery could not be used, we never heard in all our experience before.

During the heavy fighting on the left, we became engaged with the enemy in our front, driving them back, and in the evening started to the aid Hancock, but not being needed we returned to our old position.

Under cover of the night, Lee rapidly moved a heavy column forward, and hurled them on our extreme right. Our division was ordered to the support of Sedgwick, whose communication had been severed from the main army. In the darkness we felt our way cautiously, but our services were not needed, as the Sixth corps had stopped the advance of the enemy, so we returned to our former position.

And now one of the peculiar movements, from the right to the left flank commenced, preserving all the while an unbroken front.

We moved slowly during the night of the 6th, but as the new day dawned we moved faster, and by nine or ten o'clock it was a double-quick. It was said to have been a race between Grant and Lee for position at Spottsylvania Court House, and Lee won the race, securing the position, having had the inside track.

CHAPTER XI.

Spottsylvania.

THE CAVALRY struck the rebel column, and skirmished until the advance troops (5th corps) arrived, and took their place.

It was with difficulty that our division was brought into line, owing to the shattered condition of our ranks, caused by the double-quick, but a critical moment had arrived, and with a cheer the men dashed forward, re-taking the ground lost by Robinson's division. But in the charge, as usual, we advanced too far, and were in danger of being flanked, so we were ordered back to our line, where we lay on our arms till six o'clock.

The whole army had now arrived, and the order war given to advance. The enemy yielded, and the first line of entrenchments was carried, and they fell back to a strongly fortified position, from which they could not be driven. Soon after our brigade made a dash upon the enemy in our front, (unauthorized, it is said,) but there being no co-operation by other troops, we skerried back again, Col Talley commanding the brigade, and several hundred men having been taken prisoners,

At 8 a. m. on the 9th, we moved to the right-centre of the line, and were ordered to throw up Rifle-pits, which Pensyl, in the emphatic language he generally used, said, were "d—d beautiful works for somebody-else to fight behind." George uttered truthful words, if they were a little profane, for, while we built many defensive works of various kinds, I do not remember that we ever actually fought in such works.

Skirmishing. with an occasional undecisive struggle for the mastery, now continued for several days, during which we were called upon to charge on certain works in our front, but owing to the fact that every man understood that the charge was ordered as a mere feint to cover some other movement, it was not pressed.

On the 18th, we swung round to the left, and were sent forward on the skirmish line. Just in our front, possibly fifty yards off, the rebel skirmishers occupied an excellent line of rifle-pits, while we had no cover except that afforded by nature. An order was given to advance the line, which order was intended for other points on the line and not for us it seems, when John W. Shipley in the attempt to obey orders, was struck by a rebel ball, and was instantly killed. We had the satisfaction of knowing a moment later, that the same rebel was killed by Shipley's especial friend Geo. W. Pensyl. We burried Shipley near where he fell.

CHAPTER XII.

North Anna river.

GEN. LEE withdrew his forces to a strong position south of the North Anna river, and Gen'l Grant followed with the Union army in quick pursuit. We reached the river and crossed at Jericho ford on the 23rd, and spent three days in reconnoitering the position of the enemy, and then by a flank movement to the left, compelled Lee to abandon the strong position he had taken.

The Union army crossed the Pamunky river on the 28th of May, the Fifth and Ninth corps crossing at Hanover Ferry, thus bringing us once more near the locality where the terrible scenes of 1862 were enacted. Communications were opened with White-house Landing, and a new base of supplies thus secured .

Our Brigade on the 30th of May was sent out on the Mechanicsville road, near Bethesda church, to prevent a possible surprise by the enemy from that direction. Having advanced a short distance we were formed in brigade front and ordered to throw up a barricade. Company K. soon did the work that fell to their lot, and every man soon was seeking to get what rest he could, under the shade of a convenient hedge fence.

We were aroused by the sharp rattle of musketry on
both flanks of the brigade, and discovered further, that
the position had been abandoned, while we were sleeping, (an unheard-of thing, but easily explained,) and
we were seemingly, alone on the line of breast-works.
Quickly arousing the men, each hurriedly took in the
situation, then, such skedadling to the rear was never
seen before, "every man for himself, and the de'il take
the hindmost." All soon were gone except five. H. C.
Elden, Cal. Harbaugh, A. H. Blocher, G. W. Pensyl
and Capt. Minnigh, the three last named running the
risk of capture, in their efforts to induce Harbaugh and
Elden to run the gauntlet as their comrades had done.
This they refused to do, saying "I'll not do it; and be
shot down like a dog." The situation was of course an
awful one, for the rebels were now in our works on both
flanks, and the race for liberty must necessarily be in
the range of every rebel musket. Turning to Pensyl,
as the two men threw themselves on the ground, thus
deciding the question, I said, "Now let us skip out."
Geo. W. do you remember that foot-race? Hey? Do
you mind the fence, all grown up with red briars, the
"durned old haversack" filled with potatoes, that you
wanted to get rid of, and could'nt? Well, we all got
out safe, while Harbaugh and Elden were transferred
to an awful southern prison.

The Brigade now took up a new position, threw up
a barricade, and awaited the advance of the enemy,
who soon was seen, in a well dressed line of battle,
emerging from the cover of the woods, two-hundred
yards to the front. Orders were given not to fire one
shot until the enemy reached the line of an old fence
half-way across the open space between us. We never
saw so deliberate an advance by the enemy, in all our
three years experience, as this was. Brave specimen of
American soldiery they were, consciously facing death,
they came on. Two sections of a divided battery, one
on the right the other on the left, with enfilading fire,
opened on them, then the infantry added their missiles
of destruction; they come no further, a few turn and
flee to the cover of the woods, the firing ceases and an
advance is ordered, when the only enemy we find are
the torn and shapeless forms, that literally cover the
ground, they were "annihilated." (Rebel records.)

CHAPTER XIII.

Homeward bound.

HURRAH! FOR HOME. This was the glad greeting, on the morning of June 1st, when the order was issued for our return northward.

We accordingly bade farewell to the Army of the Potomac, and to the comrades of the company who had veteranized, who were now assigned to the 190th Penn'a Veteran Volunteers, to serve their unexpired term of service.

On the 2nd of June, we reached White house landing, and went aboard the transport George Weems at 10 a. m. on the 3rd, and at 12 m. with three hearty cheers, started northward, and landed at Washington, D. C. on the 4th, at 4 o'clock p. m.

On Sunday 5th at 11:30 a. m. we left the National Capitol, and on the 6th arrived at Harrisburg, Pa. the Capitol of our native State

We were the recipients of a Royal welcome when
we disembarked at Harrisburg, but the joyous greeting
can only be measured by the deep sorrow of many who
received not back their loved ones.

Three years before we as a Division of State troops,
had gone forth fully 15.000 strong, and now we were
merely a hand-full, then, full of life and buoyancy,
now, war-worn and battle-scarred veterans.

We proceeded to Philadelphia, and were finally
mustered out of the service, on the 13th of June 1864.

Company K. as a body returned to our native town
(Gettysburg,) where a Banquet welcome, had been pre-
pared for us, but owing to the fact that it was deferred
untill evening, only a few remained to partake of the
bounteous banquet, preferring the more humble spread
that awaited them, in the homes where loved ones surrounded the board.

Of the 110 who had gone forth, three years before,
only 24 now returned.

Some sleep peacefully in the unmarked graves of the
south-land ; no tender hand wreaths flowers over these
unknown graves, but the gentle zephyrs chant requiems
continually, and around them the wild flowers bloom
more beautiful and fragrant, because the soil was en-
riched by their blood. Others after a manly struggle
for life, yielded to disability from wounds and disease.

We cherish the memory of our fallen comrades, and as one by one we are summoned to join the great majority, we hope to meet them again, and to stand side by side, in nobler array, with the brave and true and tried who were our comrades here, and who so well performed their work on the battle-fields of this life.

And when the trumpet shall be heard, not calling to fields of conflict, but to rewards for deeds well done, may we all be found sharing the victory won by Him, "who died that we might live."

Historical Record

OF THE MEMBERS

Of Co. K. Ist P. R. V. C.

AUTHOR'S PREFACE.

While it is somewhat of a delicate matter, to write up this Historical Record of individuals, yet we think it should be a part of the purpose intended by this volume. We take up the membership of the company, according to rank: First, the Commissioned Officers, in the order of seniority; Second, the non-Commissioned officers, as found on the rolls at date of muster out; Third, the members of the company in alphabetical order.

HISTORICAL RECORD.

Captain Edward McPherson.

To Captain McPherson, presumably, belongs the credit of organizing Company K. He served as its commander until August 24th, 1861, when he resigned, to take his seat in the First Session of the Thirty-seventh Congress, which convened at Washington, on the 4th of July 1861. On the adjournment of that body, he reported for duty, as a volunteer aid on the staff of Gen'l McCall, commanding the Penn'a Reserves, and served as such until November, when the Second session of said congress convened. While a Staff-officer, he was a convenient intermediary, between the Division and the Executive department at Washington, to which he had ready access by reason of his representative capacity.

Being Inspector general on the staff, he visited each Regiment and Battery of the command, and reported its condition as to organization, health, arms and efficiency, which report was transmitted regularly each week, to army Head-quarters. During his term as congressman he was a member of the committe on military affairs. He was Clerk of the House of Representatives, after his term as a member expired, and is now serving in that capacity. His residence, when at home, is Gettysburg, Pa.

Captain J. Findley Bailey.

At the organization of the company Capt. Bailey was made 1st Lieutenant, and succeeded McPherson, to the Captaincy, to date September 1st 1861.

Bailey was a born soldier, a strict disciplinarian, at all times seemingly stern, yet easily approached, and much beloved by every one.

At the battle of Charles city cross roads, June 30th 1862, he led the company in a general charge against the enemy. When last seen he was pressing forward in pursuit of fleeing foe, and when the recall was sound·ed, Capt. Bailey did not return. and from that hour to the present he has never been heard of. What his fate was, we dare scarcely permit ourselves even to guess. But if he fell, it was facing the foe, and doing noble service, and dying a soldiers glorious death.

Captain W. Warren Stewart.

Captain Stewart was made Orderly Sergeant of the company at its organization, and served as such until the promotion attending the resignation of Mc-Pherson took place, when he was chosen 1st Lieuten-ant, to date September 3rd 1861. Soon afterward he was appointed Adjutant of the Regiment, and served as such until June 30th 1862, when he was severely wounded, and was finally sent to the Gen'l Hospital, at David's Island, N. Y. where he remained until the early part of October following, when he returned to the company encamped at Sharpsburg, Md. During his absence from the company he was promoted to the Captaincy, vice Bailey, who was reported killed, and mustered to date June 30th 1862. He now remained in command of the company until the general promo-tion took place in the early part of 1863, when he was commissioned Lieut. Colonel, to date March 7th 1863.

Stewart had a firm hold upon the hearts and affections of the whole regiment, and as he served in a regimental capacity most of the time, he was popular in the Division. While he was qualified to command, he possessed, at the same time, excellent clerical and executive ability. He was mustered out with the regiment, June 13. 1864, and soon after was appointed Colonel, and had command of the 112th Regiment, Penn'a Volunteers, which position he held to the close of the war. Professionally, he is a civil engineer, and finds constant employment in that vocation.

His residence and P. O. address is York Springs, Pa.

Captain Henry N. Minnigh.

Capt. Minnigh recorded his name on the register of the company only a few hours before it left Gettysburg, and therefore had no part in the "getting up" of Co. K, having enlisted as "a high private in the rear rank." When the company was fully organized at Camp Wayne, he was appointed Fourth Serg't, and at Camp Tennally, September 3. 1861, he was promoted to Orderly Sergeant, by Col. R. Biddle Roberts, and held the position till after the Peninsula campaign.

He was promoted to 2nd Lieut. and was mustered as such, to date June 30. 1862. Immediately after his promotion, he was ordered to report to the officer in charge of the Division ambulance corps, for duty with said corps, but by special request he was excused from that duty, and he remained with the company.

Frequently, was it made the especial work of Capt. Minnigh, to be sent out on a scouting expedition, or a reconnoisance with a detail of picked men, and he can recount some daring and dangerous adventures, through which he passed while performing such duty.

At the battle of South mountain September 14. '62, he was wounded by a minnie ball, through the left arm near the shoulder, at the same instant that Lieut. Sadler was killed, thus leaving the company without a commissioned officer. He was absent. from the command, just three weeks.

On March 7. 1863, he was promoted to 1st Lieut. and on October 27. to Captain, both commissions are however dated March 7.

In reference to Capt. Minnigh's character as a soldier and a commanding officer, we quote from manuscripts in our possession. Rob't T. McKinney says, "I can never forget the Captain's kindness of heart,

Minnigh.

when in the service. Doubtless, he will remember how, when on the march, he used to come from the right of the company to the left where I was, and kindly, ask how I was pulling through, then seeing my feeble condition, he demanded my arms and equipments, and and also the knapsack, strapped them on his own tired body, and then ordering me to march outside of the ranks, took his place in the company, and carred my burdens through a weary march for 48 hours."

Wm. T Jobe says, " As a soldier, Cap't Minnigh's record is an enviable one, he led the company with gallantry and spirit on all occasions, securing the commendations of his superior officers, for bravery and good behavior, under trying circumstances."

He is the possessor of a commission as Brev.- Major, signed by the President of the United States.

Having been mustered out with the company, June 13. 1864, he prceeded to Washington, and accepted a clerkship in the War department, where he served till August 9. 1866, when he returned to his native county and engaged in teaching.

In the spring of 1871, he entered the ministry of the Methodist Episcopal church, and has been laboring successfully in the Itinerancy since that time.

Lieut. J. Durbin Sadler.

Lieutenant Sadler at the organization of the company was appointed First Corporal. August 22. he was chosen 2nd Lieut. vice Herron resigned, and served as such until September 30. 1862, when he was appointed 1st Lieut. to succeed Stewart promoted.

It is sad to record the sacrifice of one who lived so noble a life, for when Lieut. Sadler fell, the company we think, lost its best commanding officer. Sadler was killed by a minnie ball, in the battle of South mountain September 14. 1862, while gallantly leading the command in the final charge, which drove the enemy from the summit and gave the victory to our forces.

His body was removed to his home at York springs, Pa. and was buried with the honors of war, under the charge of Lieut. Minnigh, who in his wounded state accompanied his remains and laid them to rest.

He sleeps peacefully by the side of his ancestors, in the beautiful cemetery at Hampden, Pa. awaiting a glorious resurrection, which his pure and spotless life and character warrants. May we meet him again on the peaceful shore, beyond life's troubled river.

Lieut. George E. Kitzmiller.

At the age of Twenty-one years Lieut. Kitzmiller entered the service as a private, at the organization of the company, and was made 7th Corporal on the 3rd day of September 1861. November 1st '62, he was promoted to Orderly Sergeant, vice Minnigh, and on March 7th 1863, he was mustered as 2nd Lieut. and finally as 1st Lieut. October 1st 1863.

He was mustered out with the company, June 13th 1864, returned to his home at Gettysburg and there followed the business of Granite cutting for several years. He died on the 12th day of March 1874.

Lieut. Kitzmiller was a good officer, was well liked by all, and looked well after the interests of the company, in whatever capacity he served.

Lieut. J. J. Herron.

Lieut. Herron was an Attorney at Gettysburg, when the company was formed, and was elected to the office of 2nd Lieutenant.

On August 17. just when we were called into active service he resigned. It was reported that he subsequently did good service in the army elsewhere.

Lieut. John C. Brandon.

At the organization of the company, J. C Brandon enlisted as a private, and on November 1st 1862, he was promoted to 5th Sergeant. October 1st '63, he was made 2nd Sergeant, and soon afterward on recommendation, received a commission as 2nd Lieut. but was never mustered as such, owing to the fact that the company was below the minimum in number.

Sergt. Brandon was detailed with the Ambulance corps, in June '63, and again in April '64, and was also for a short time, at Regimental Head-quarters, on detailed duty. He was mustered out with the company June 13. 1864, when he returned home and engaged in farming. Eventually he drifted westward and located at Salt springs, Missouri.

Samuel A. Young, Orderly Sergt.

Samuel A. Young, was a Drug clerk at the outbreak of the war, and at the age of twenty, enlisted on June 8, 1861. His promotions, date as follows:— 5th corporal July 26. 1861, 3rd corporal November 1. '62, Orderly sergt. March 7. 1863.

Young.   McGonigle.

Sergt. Young filled well every position in which he was placed, and as an Orderly he was a treasure. The books were neatly kept and always at hand, as he had a habit of carrying those most needed in his knapsack.

He was wounded near Fredericsburg, early in '62, by the accidental discharge of his musket. For some time he was detailed as Sergeant of the guard at Gen'l Reynold's head-quarters, and was also detailed on recruiting service under Capt. Dobson. He was mustered out with the company, and soon afterward found his way to the west, and located in Iowa; he is growing up with the country, and is in the Merchantile business at Penora, Guthrie Co. Iowa.

James McGonigle. 2nd Sergeant.

James McGonigle, entered the service as a private at the organization of the company, being nineteen years of age and a mason by trade. On November 1st '62, he was promoted to 2nd Corporal, and March 1st '63, to 2nd Sergeant. As a non-commissioned officer he attended strictly to his duty, and was honorably mustered out with the company. We believe he is still living, but we could not secure his present address.

Peter S. Harbaugh. 3rd Sergeant.

At the age of twenty-two, Sergt. Harbaugh joined
the company as a volunteer, at Camp Tennally Sep't
20. 1861. November 1. '62, he was made 6th Corporal,
and October 1. '63, 3rd Sergeant.

February 10th '64, he re-enlisted, and took sick
when home on veteran furlough, but when sufficiently
recovered, reported to Camp distribution, and was at
once sent to Auger Gen'l hospital, Va. In the hospital
he was placed on duty in the laundry, and remained
there till Feb'y 9. '65, when he was discharged on a
surgeons certificate of disability. He is constantly a
sufferer, on account of the disability contracted in the
service. Address, — Fairfield, Adams Co. Pa.

Michael M. Miller. 4th Sergeant.

Michael M. Miller, a citizen of Gettysburg and a
Painter by occupation, was recruited June 28. '61; he
was promoted to 3rd Corporal November 1. '62, and
to 4th Sergeant March 7. '63. Being mustered out with
the company, he returned to Gettysburg, and followed
his trade. He died August 5. 1877.

Hamilton.	Beamer.	Culbertson.

Joseph Hamilton. 1st Corporal.

Hamilton was a volunteer recruit, September 3rd 1861. On November 1 '62, he was promoted to 8th Corporal, and on October 1. '63, to 1st Corporal.

Joe was a No 1. soldier, and could be depended on under any circumstance. At the battle of Mechanics-ville June 26. '62, he was severely wounded, and was sent to the Gen'l hospital from wich he returned Sept. 27, '63. At the muster out of the company he was trans-ferred to the 190. Penn'a V. Volunteers, to serve the unexpired term. Address :— Seven Stars, Pa.

Harry H. Beamer. 2nd Corporal.

Beamer joined the company at its organization, and was made 2nd Corporal March 7, '63. He was a soldier that "never shirked duty, and was always on hand." At the muster out of the company he retired to his home near Gettysburg, and finally went west.

James F. Culbertson. 3rd Corporal.

Culbertson was one of the original members of the company, and was made 3rd Corporal March 7, 1863. He was severely wounded at Gettysburg July 3, '63. Jim was a good soldier. P. O. address:— York, Pa.

Carson.	Baker.	Mackley.

George O. Carson. 4th Corporal.

Carson, entered the service with company as a private, and was promoted to 4th Corporal, March 7, 1863. He was wounded at Gaines' Hill, during the Seven day's battles, and was finally mustered out with the company. "Kit" was a valiant soldier, and did his work well in all the sphere of soldierly warfare; he dearly loved a cup of hot coffee, and knew how to get the best the sutler or commissary afforded.

He still enjoys the good things of life, and for substantial proof, call on him at Uriah P. O. Cumberland County, Penn'a.

Joseph S. Baker. 5th Corporal.

Baker, entered the service July 19. '61, leaving his vocation, that of Brick-laying, for his country's service. He was made 5th Corporal, March 7. '63, veteranized, February 10. '64, and was transferred to the 190 P. V. Vol's, at the muster out of the company.

John F. Mackley. 6th Corporal.

Mackley, enlisted June 8. '61, at the age of twenty, and was promoted to 6th Corporal, March 7, '63.

He was mustered out with the company, and now resides in the oil regions of Penn'a.

Robert T. McKinney. 7th Corporal.

McKinney, was a volunteer recruit, mustered in on August 28. '61, and was made 7th Corporal, October 1, '63. During the term of service he was several times detailed on duty with the Division provost guard.

At the muster out of the company he was transferred to the 190 P. V. Vol's, to serve the unexpired term, and was mustered out on the battle-field, near reams station, Va. August 27, 1864. In 1876, he entered the ministry of the Baptist church but on account of failing health was compelled to leave the work. He is now serving his second enlistment, and is at this time, the Orderly of Co. D. 12th Reg't, N. G. of Penn'a. Address :— Williamsport, Pa.

Andrew A. Slagle. 8th Corporal.

Slagle, was one of the original members of Co. K, and was promoted 8th Corporal to date, October 1. '63. We cheerfully record the fact, that Slagle was one of our most moral and upright men, and a model of piety under every circumstance, and while he was one of our oldest members, his influence was most salutary in restraining the younger. He was mustered out with the company, and resides at Hanover, Pa.

Gilbert.   Arendt.   Beales.

Charles E. Gilbert. Musician.

Enlisted June 8. 1861. Age 22, and a coach- maker by trade. Was a Drummer from the beginning to the ending of the war. Re-enlisted on February 10. '64, and was transferred to the 190 Pa. Vet. Vol's, at the muster out of the company, and was finally discharged July 3. '65. Charlie frequently did duty in assisting the wounded on the battle field, but always claimed that he enlisted as a musician. Since his service ended, he has been a guide on the Battle-field of Gettysburg.

— *Arendt Jacob,* was a volunteer recruit September 4, '61. He was a good soldier, and was wounded at Gettysburg on the second day. At muster out of the company he was transferred to the 190 Pa. Vet. Vol's, to serve the unexpired term, and died soon after the war, but unfortunately, we have no dates.

— *Beales Charles W.* joined the company at its origin, was then nineteen years of age and a miller by occupation. He was mustered out with the company, and resides at York Springs, Penn'a.

— *Beard Obadiah M.* enlisted June 8. '61, was a harness-maker by trade, and 33 years of age. On February 10. '64, he re-enlisted, and when the company was mustered out he was transferred to the 190 Pa. v. vol's. We have entirely lost sight of Beard, and know not whether he be living or dead.

— *Bingaman Samuel,* went out with the company, and did good service; he was on detailed service for a while with the provost-guard in August '63, and was mustered out with the company.

— *Bingaman David,* was one of original company, and did his duty well until October 24. '62, when he deserted, and never returned to the company.

— *Blocher Andrew H.* was recruited July 19, '61. He was taken prisoner in the evening of June 30. '62, and exchanged in July. Was on detailed service for a while in July '63. In February '64, he desired to re-enlist, but did not pass examination. At muster out of the company he returned to his home at Bendersville, Penn'a, where he now resides.

☞ Andy was the best sharp-shooter in Co, K. ☜

Brandon.	Cassatt.	Caufman Wm. H.

— *Brandon Isaac M.*, age twenty years, a farmer by occupation, enlisted June 8. '61, and was promoted 7th Corporal July 26. '61, and to 1st Corporal Sept. 1, '61. He lost his rank when he peitioned for a transfer to another command, and said transfer was made by order of the Secretary of war, January 15. '63, to Co. H, 2nd Batt. 12th U. S. I. to serve the unexpired term, and was finally mustered out June 8. '64. Address :— Paola, Kansas.

— *Cassatt Samuel J*, enlisted June 8. '61, was 19 years of age, and a Shoemaker by trade. He was very severely wounded on June 30. '62, and returned from General hospital November 13, '62. Re-enlisted February 10. '64, and at muster out of the company was transferred to the 190 Pa. Vet. Vol's.

— *Caufman Wm. H.* age 24, and by occupation a clerk, enlisted June 8, '61. Was made 8th corporal on July 26, and 4th corporal September 3, '61.

On account of disability we presume, he went to the hospital at David's Island N Y. and remained there in some capacity from July 9. '62, till muster out of the company.

— *Bailey Daniel D.* enlisted June 8. '61, was made a Corporal, and on September 1. '61, was transferred to the 12th Penn'a Reserves.

— *Caufman Charles E.* aged twenty-two years, a farmer by occupation, enlisted June 8. '61. At Charles City cross roads he was badly wounded, and fell into the hands of the enemy. His leg was amputated and having been exchanged as a prisoner, he was discharged November 3. '62, by order of Brig.-Gen'l Harvey Brown.

— *Chronister Amos*, went out at the organization of the company, was a farmer, and twenty-two years of age. By Spec. order No. 28, Hd, qr, First brigade, he was detailed with the ammunition train as a driver. Feb'y 3. '64 but soon returned to the co. by spec. order. Re-enlisted February 10. '64, and at muster out of the co. was transferred to the 190 Pa. Vet. Vol's.

— *Cox George W.* was recruited July 19. '61, was a farmer, and 19 years of age. He served continuously with the co. and was mustered out with it, June 13, 1864. He was one of our quiet and steady members.

Creamer.   Devine.   Dixon Wm.   Dixon Sam'l.

— *Creamer John T.* enlisted June 8. '61, was a coach-maker aged 29 years. Served with the company till after the battle of Gettysburg, and was then sent to Mt. Pleasant Gen'l hospital, Washington, D. C. where he died, December 21. 1863.

— *Devine Bernard*, joined June 8. '61, was a farmer, and 39 years of age. He was detached with Battery A. Penn'a Reserve artillery, by Spec. order, No. 78. April 2. '62, where he served till mustered out on account of disability, February 19, 1863.

Barney was the only Irishman in the company.

— *Dixon William*, was a member of the company from the beginning, age 19 years and by occupation a laborer. Was discharged, December 24. 1861, on account of physical disability.

— *Dixon Samuel*, a brother of Wm. also was a member of the original company, age eightteen years and a laborer by occupation. Was detailed with the provost guard July 29. '63, for a brief space, and was finally mustered out with the company.

Nothing foolish about Sammy, but he was always there.

Duey.	Danner.	Durboraw.

— *Duey John J.* joined the company at its origin, and was made 2nd Sergeant. He deserted from camp at Shargsburg, Md. and was reduced to the ranks, by order of Col. Roberts October 17. '62, and December 29, returned to the company. In the Wilderness campaign he was notably brave and daring, and on the 16th of May near Spottsylvania, he was very severely wounded by a minnie ball, and was sent to the hospital. We heard that he died there, but no official notice of such fact was ever received. On December 29. '63, he re-enlisted as a veteran volunteer.

— *Danner H. Knox,* was a member of the company at its organization, and was made 7th Corporal Nov. 1. '62, but on account of contin ed absence from the command, being sick in Gen'l hospital from July '62, to January '64, he was deposed from office. Is still suffering on account of disability contracted by a sunstroke, during the Peninsula campaign. Was mustered out with the company and resides at York, Penn'a.

— *Durboraw Isaac N.* went out with the company at its original organization, and was promoted to 6th Corporal July 26. '61, and 4th Sergeant Nov. 1, '62.

Durboraw.

Durboraw was a sympathetic man, and as such was always ready to assist the helpless; he took charge of Wisotskey when he received his terrible wound, and with the assistance of Beales, carried him from the field, and when he died, as the shades of evening fell, they scooped a grave and buried him; he also assisted in carrying Lt.-Col. McIntyre from the field, when he received the wound, from which he afterward died. He was slightly wounded at Charles City cross roads, and by an accidental injury May 19. '63, when he was hit on the foot by a 12 pound cannon ball, tossed by some one, from which injury he has never fully recovered.

He applied for a transfer and was reduced to the ranks, on October 1. '63, and was finally transferred to the Signal Corps, by Spec. order, No. 317, Head quarters Army of the Potomac, November 1, 1863.

On June 9. '64, he was discharged by reason of expiration of term, when he returned to his home, and resumed farming; has been a Surveyor and a Justice of the Peace for 25 years, and resides at the Durboraw homestead, in Mountjoy Township, Adams Co., Penn'a. Address:– Two Taverns, Pa.

☞ We are under especial obligation, to comrade Durboraw for valuable assistance in this work.

(See reminiscences.)

— *Elden Henry W. C*, was recruited July 26, 1861.
The recruiting officer (Sergt. Minnigh) refused to ac-
cept him, being only 16 years of age, but he followed
to camp, and reporting his age as 18 years, was mustered in. Though "Doc" was an excellent soldier, we
must nevertheless record the fact of his being reported
a deserter, not having returned to the company, when
absence with leave expired. August 30. '63, he was
sent back under arrest, having been absent from July
6, '63. Charges were necessarily preferred, but by a
special request made by Capt. Minnigh, he was releas-
ed from arrest and all charges were withdrawn, on the
29th of Oct, 1863. He re-enlisted as a Vet. Volunteer December 29, 1863. At the battle of Bethesda
church, June 30. '64, he was taken prisoner, (See page
37,) and endured the horrors of Libby, Andersonville
and Florence prisons, and died at the last named
place, but we failed in securing dates.

— *Eyster Samuel H.* aged 19, and a Silver smith
by trade, was recruited July 19, '61. He was wounded at South mountain, September 14. '62, and was discharged from the service, at Frederick, Md, January
19, '63, by order of Thos. S. McKenzie.

— *Fanus Hiram J.* a laborer aged 20 years, joined the company at its organization. On March 25. 1863, he was discharged on account of physical disability, at Phil'a, and now resides at Idaville, Pa.

— *Foutz Adam,* age 20, a laborer, enlisted June 28. '61, and deserted September 13. '62, arrested and seet back to the co. tried by court-martial, spec. order No. 10, Div. Hd-qrs, March 9. '64, and sentenced to forfeit all pay due, and $10 per month for ballance of his term, and to make up lost time, equivalent to, 13 mo. and 25 days. Was transferred to the 190 P. V. V. to serve the unexpired term.

— *Gardner Richard P.* was recruited July 19. '61, was a coach-maker and 21 years of age. Deserted from hospital at Annapolis, December 16. '63, and never returned to the company.

— *Gardner Amos F.* enlisted June 8. '61, aged 21, and a farmer by occupation. He deserted from Gen'l hospital at Washington, D. C. March 3. '63, was returned under arrest. February 12. '64, and at muster out of company was transferred to 190 P. V. Vol's.

Gibbs.	Hamilton C.	Hart B.	Hart L. J.

— *Gibbs George W.* aged 20 years, a wheel-wright by trade, joined the company at its organization; he was an excellent soldier, and he always was ready for duty; served the whole term, and was mustered out with the company.

— *Hamilton Calvin,* was a volunteer recruit, Sept. 4. '62. He was detailed with the ambulance corps, December 8. '62, and did excellent service with said corps at the battle of Fredericksburg, Dec. 13, 1862.

He was severely wounded at Gettysburg, July 2 '63, in the charge made by the Penn'a Reserves, and was on account of said wounds, transferred to Co. D, 12th Veteran Reserves, January 13. '63, and was discharg- at Point Lookout, June 29, '65. He is a Teacher pro-fessionally, and since Sept. 1889, he has been Supt. of the Gettysburg National Cemetery.

— *Hart Barnett,* enlisted June 8. '61, aged 39 yrs, and a mason by trade. Deserted, from Brooks station Va. December 26. '62, and never returned to the co.

— *Hart Levi J.* aged 27 years, and a mason by oc-cupation, went out with the company. On June 16. '62, he was discharged at Camp Pierpont, Va. on account of physical disability.

— *Harbaugh Calvin,* enlisted June 8, 1861. Aged 19 years, and by profession a laborer. Re-enlisted Feb'y 10, '64. Was taken prisoner, May 30. '64, (see page 37,) and at muster out of co. was transferred to the 190 P. V. Vol's. Was in Libby prison, and when Lee surrendered, he was at Andersonville. Returned home in June 1865, went to Kansas in 1867, and died soon afterward.

— *Henry Peter H.* enlisted at the origin of the company, was 24 years of age, and by trade a miller. He was made 3rd Sergeant, and promoted to 2nd Serg't Nov. 1. '62, and soon afterward reduced to the ranks for insubordination, by order of Col. Roberts. Was wounded at South mountain Sept. 14. '62, and discharged January 10. '63, at Frederick, Md.

— *Hildebrand John F.* joined at organization, was 19 years of age, and professionally a bar-keeper. He deserted from Gen'l hospital Washington, D. C. March 3. '63, and never returned to the company.

— *Hollinger Philip,* a black-smith, aged 30, joined June 8. '61, and was discharged December 22. '61, at Camp Pierpont, Va. on account of disability.

— *Hortkins Henry*, enlisted July 19. '61, age 37 years, and a cabinet-maker by trade. The muster out roll reports him, previously discharged, but no dates are given.

— *Houck Philip L.* enlisted June 8. 1861, and was made 2nd Corporal, and September 3. '61, was promoted to 5th Sergeant. At Charles City cross roads, June 30. '62, he was severely wounded, and was discharged, September 12, '62. He afterward was elected to represent his native county, (Adams) in the Legislature. P. O. address, Gettysburg, Pa.

— *Jacobs John H. K.* was 20 years of age, a plasterer by trade, enlisted June 8, 1861. Was on detailed service with the Pioneer corps March 1864, and was much absent from the company on account of physical disability. After his muster out with the company, he resided at Shenandoah, Pa. till '76, when he went to Council Bluffs, Iowa, and to Omaha, Neb. in 1881, where he died February 3. 1891.

— *Jobe William T.* went out with the company, in his 19th year and was a Blacksmith by trade; he was a true soldier; we think he never was absent from the co.

Johns.	Jones.	Keckler.	Keim.

He was mustered out with the company, and at the present time holds a position in the Revenue service of the U. S. government. Address:– York Springs., Pa.

— *Johns David E.* was a laborer, 18 years of age when he joined the company, at its first organization.

Dave was a little unruly sometimes, but withall was a good soldier: he stuck to the company and was mustered out with it.

— *Jones Henry H.* joined the company June 14. '61, and deserted near Waterford, Va., November 1. '62, was returned to the co, under arrest, August 30, '63. Re-enlisted Feb. 10. '64, and while on veteran furlough deserted again, and was never heard of afterward. The muster roll says he was from Kentucky.

— *Keckler Samuel,* a blacksmith by trade, aged 19 years, enlisted September 3, '61. Re-enlisted as a Vet. volunteer December 29, '63, and at muster out of the company was transferred to the 190 P. V. Vols.

— *Keim Frederick A.* aged 22; a mason by trade; went out with the company at its organization. The rolls report him as having died at U. S. hospital, Baltimore, Md. No date given.

— *Lady Hiram,* joined the company Sept. 3, 1861.
Age 19, and a carpenter by trade. Was wounded at
Charles City cross roads, taken prisoner, exchanged
and discharged at Annapolis, April 16, 1863.

— *Leech Elijah L.* a farmer; age 19 years: enlisted
September 4, '61. Was a teamster at Brig. Hospital,
for ten weeks from November 16, '63. Re-enlisted as
a Vet. Volunteer, Dec. 29, '63, and at muster out of
the co. was transferred to the 190 P. V. Vols.

— *Mackley Jacob,* enlisted June 8. 1861, was a laborer by occupation, and 23 years of age. Jake spent
considerable of his time in the guard-house, but was
finally mustered out with the company.

— *Megary William R.* went out at the organization
of the company; age 21 years, and a manufacturer by
trade. Was on detail with the Pioneer corps, August
3, '63, and with the Provost-guard January 4, 1864,
and while on the first named detail was slightly wounded by a spent ball. He was mustered out with the co.
and since that time has resided at Hazleton, Pa, and
has been an engineer on the Lehigh valley R. R. for
twenty years.

McGrew.   McKinney.   Miller.   Metcalf.

— *McGrew William*, age 22; a shoe-maker by profession, enlisted September 4, 1862. He was severely wounded at Gettysburg July 2, '63, and died at the Hospital, July 6, '63. He is buried in the National cemetery at that place.

— *McKinney John W.* enlisted August 22, 1861. A farmer and 18 years of age. Was a good soldier but yielded to disability brought on by exposure and died at the Gen'l hospital Alexandria, Va., Feb'y 24, 1863. He is also buried in the Nat. Cemetery at Gettysburg.

— *Miller Peter W.* was a recruit July 19, '61, was a farmer aged 18 years. He fell in the battle of South mountain, September 14, 1862.

> "With latest breath, ... he cried,
> 'Bear up the Flag,' —— and died."

— *Metcalf Wooster B.* was one of the original company, aged 20, and a clerk by profession. Was wounded accidentally during the Peninsula campaign, and went to the Hospital at Phil'a, where he remained till January '63, when he left, and from that date he was reported as a deserter. Residence :– Hanover, Pa.

-- *Monteer Henry R.* joined the company July 24, '61; age 21 and a sadler by trade. Detailed at Div. head-quarters as Sadler, March 7, '64, S. O. No, 74. Re-enlisted December 29, '63, and was at muster out of the co. transferred to the 190 P. V. Vol's.

-- *Mumper William,* went out with the company; was 19 years of age and a farmer by occupation.
Re-enlisted Feb'y 10, '64, and transferred finally to the 190 P. V. Vol's. Will was one of our best men, and a terrible fellow in the excitement of battle. At battle of Charles City cross roads, he was severely wounded. Address :– Sheridan Lake-side, Nebraska.

-- *Myers David M.* age 21; a clerk; enlisted June 8, '61. On November 1, '63, he was transferred to the Non-commissioned staff, and we think re-enlisted as a Veteran volunteer.

-- *Myers John J.* was one of the original company, age 21 and a clerk by profession. On account of physical disability, he was discharged at Camp Pierpont, December 22, '61, and died several years ago at his home in Gettysburg.

Myers G. W.	Nailor.	Naylor.	Ogden.

— *Myers George W.* enlisted September 3, '61, was a carpenter, and 20 years of age. Died of disease at Camp Pierpont, December 3, '61, and was sent home for burial.

— *Nailor Wilson E.* came to Camp Wayne when only sixteen years of age, but reported himself as nineteen, and was mustered in July 19, '61. At Gettysburg, in the evening of second day, he was wounded, and was at Gen'l hospital till October 23, when he returned to the company. Re-enlisted on February 10, '64, and at muster out of co, was transferred to the 190 P. V. Vol's. At present he resides in Harrisburg, and is a Dentist by profession.

— *Naylor Jeremiah E.* was recruited July 19, '61, at nineteen years of age, and a laborer by occupation. At the battle of South mountain, September 14, 1862, he was killed instantly by a minnie ball. "The noblest fell that day."

— *Ogden John Q.* age 18; a farmer; enlisted Sept. 4, '62, did good service, and at muster out of the co, was transferred to the 190 Pa. V. Volunteers, to serve the unexpired term of service.

Pearce.	Pensyl.	Pittenger.	Rhodes.

— *Pearce J. Shaw,* age 20; a butcher; enlisted on Sept. 3, '61. Was discharged for disability, October 3, '63, from Convalescent camp by order of General Martindale. Resides in Washington, D. C. where he is in Government employ.

— *Pensyl George W.* age 20; a plasterer by trade; enlisted June 8, '61. He was detached on recruiting service, June 12, '63, and re-enlisted February 10, '64, and transferred finally to the 190 P. V. Vol's. George was as good a soldier as ever carried a musket, and he was always disposed to make the best out of every situation. Resides at Bendersville, Pa.

— *Pittenger John F.* was one of the original company was a laborer by occupation, 25 years of age. He was a good soldier, and re-enlisted on February 10,'64, and at muster out of co, was transferred to the 190 P. V. Vol's.

— *Rhodes Andrew H.* was recruited July 24, '61; a clerk; and 21 years of age. Was discharged from Gen'l hospital at Alexandria, Feb'y 11, '63. Resides at York Springs, Pa.

Riggs.	Remmel.	Resser.	Robison.

— *Riggs William A.* went out with the company; age 18: a shoe-maker by profession. He was detailed with the Pioneer corps, from June 26, '63, to July 30, '63; and was mustered out with the company.

— *Remmel David E. H.* was one of the original co, was a laborer by occupation, 18 years of age. Was detailed with the Ambulance corps, September 15, 1863, and was mustered out with the company.

— *Resser Jacob,* was one of the original company, a merchant; 40 years of age. At organization he was made 3rd Corporal, and was appointed to receive and distribute the mail, and served in said capacity at Camp Wayne, Tennally and Pierpont; he also had charge of all express matter. He was promoted to Qr. master Sergeant, by Col. Roberts, and transferred to the Non-commissioned Staff, March 26, 1862, and was mustered out June 13, 1864. He is now engaged in the Tin and Stove business at East Berlin, Pa.

— *Robison Daniel W.* age 23; a tailor by trade was a member of the company from its organization. Was detailed as Regimental tailor, September 14, '63, and was employed as such until the campaign of '64.

Rosensteel.	Rouzer.	Shaffer.

"Web, was always up to something," says Orderly Young, "but the failure to capture a whole barrel of ham, at Brooks station, must be recorded against him." Resides at Punxsutawney, Jefferson Co., Pa.

— *Rosensteel John H.* age 21; a farmer; enlisted June 8, '61, re-enlisted December 29, '63, and served the company well till muster out, when he and transferred finally to the 190 P. V. Vol's.

— *Rouzer James M.* age 40; a carpenter; enlisted July 19, '61. Went home on furlough May 27, '63, and having taken sick while there, was absent quite a long time, but returned in season to join in the wilderness campaign. "Snap" was a peculiar sort of a soldier, but the strangest thing he did, and perhaps the only occurrence of the kind on record, took place at the battle of the Wilderness, when he actually caught a minnie ball in his mouth, after it had knocked out two of his front teeth. He was mustered out with the company, and died at Gettysburg, July 25, 1885.

— *Shaffer David*, age 18; a farmer; joined Sept. 3, 1861, and was discharged December 4, '63, on account of physical disability. Address :– Markle, Indiana.

Shank.	Sheads.	Shipley.

— *Shank Jesse* enlisted June 8, '61, at the age 24, and was a shoe-maker by trade. He died of disease at Camp Pierpont, Va., November 24, '61, and was sent home for burial.

— *Sheads Robert,* went out with the company, was 18 years of age and a machinist by trade. Reported a deserter on route to Gettysburg June 26, '63, and then reported himself to the Gen'l hospital at that place, as sick, was furloughed for 20 days, from October 3, to 23, '63, when he returned to the company. Re-enlisted, December 29, '63, and was at muster out transferred to the 190 P. V. Vol's. He is dead, we believe.

— *Shipley John W.* joined the company July 24, 1861, was a teamster, aged 24 years. He was killed at Spottsylvania, on wednesday May 18, '64, while doing noble duty on the skirmish line. The comrades buried him under the wide-spread branches of an evergreen.

> Breathe soft, ye winds!
> Ye waters, gently flow!
> Shield him, oh, evergreen!
> Ye flowers, around him grow!
> Unhallowed feet, I beg you pass in silence by!
> Our Comrade here asleep doth lie.

Siplinger.	Stewart.	Stouffer.	Swisher.

— *Siplinger Mathias J.* age 18 ; a farmer; enlisted July 19, '61. Was absent much in Hospital, and was discharged May 7, '63, on account of physical disability, by order of Gen'l Heintzelman.
We know not whether he is dead or living

— *Stewart David M.* age 20 ; a farmer; enlisted June 8, '61, and served on detail at Gen'l hospital in Baltimore, from October 10, '62, till muster out.
We are not advised as to his present residence.

— *Stouffer Jacob,* enlisted June 8, '61, at the age of 27, and was a shoe-maker by trade. Was taken prisoner November 27, '63, while disobeying orders, and he was mustered out with the company in his absence.

— *Swisher Charles A.* age 20 ; a stone-cutter; joined July 19, 1861. Deserted on route to Gettysburg June 26, '63, and then reported himself to the Gen'l hospital at Phil'a August 19, '63, and was returned to the company. January 15, '64, he was transferred to the Invalid corps. Resides at Pine-grove, Cumb'd co, Pa.

— *Tawney Charles Z.* was 29 years of age, and a brick-layer by trade; joined the company, June 28, 1861. Was made 8th Corporal, August 24, 1861, and promoted to 5th, September 3, '62, and discharged for disability, January 2, '63. Resides at Gettysburg, Pa.

— *Trimmer William,* age 18; a farmer; enlisted July 19, '61. He was discharged November 3, '62, on account of physical disability, (deafness,) contracted under the heavy cannonry, in the Peninsula campaign. He afterward served as cook, for the officers of Co. I, 205 P. V. In 1872, went to Kansas, and took a homestead, but returned to Penn'a in 1883. He now resides at Mechanicsburg, Pa.

— *Weber Frank,* enlisted June 8, '61, at the age of 21, and was a tobacconist by trade. Deserted December 12, '62, from Brooks station, Va., and never was seen afterward. He was a "Baltimore dutchman."

— *Wisotzkey Craig F.* age 20; a Coach-painter; enlisted June 8, '61. He was killed at Mechanicsville in the battle of June 26, 1862, and was the first of the company that fell in the country's service. The comrades buried him near the battle field.

Woodring.   Woods.   Goutermuth.   Sheets.

—. *Woodring David H.* one of the original co, was a lime-burner by occupation, 27 years of age. Was detailed with the Pioneer corps, in July 1863. Re-enlisted as a Vet. volunteer February 10, '64, and was at muster out of the co. transferred to the 190 P. Vet. Vol's. Residence, Lancaster, Pa.

— *Woods Alex. L. C.* age 25 ; a cabinet-maker by trade, was a member of the company from its organization. Was made 5th Sergeant, July 26, '61, and promoted to 4th Sergeant, September 3, '61. Discharged on account of physical disability, but no official notice was ever received. He died a few years ago, in the west, where his family now resides.

— *Goutermuth Paul* and *Sheets Samuel,* were on the original rolls of the co, but were not actually mustered into the U. S. service. They were however arrested as deserters, in 1863, sent back to the co. Court-martialed and sentenced to serve the full term, and at muster out of the co. were transferred to the 190 P. Veteran Volunteers. These men we believe suffered unjustly, as they never were recognized as members of the company, and were not reported as deserters from it.

Several other names.

— *John Gibson, Adam Holtzworth, George Holtz-worth, Zephaniah Rogers, William Zell and Geo. Little,* when the company was mustered into the U. S. service at Camp Carroll Baltimore, Md., July 26, '61, stepped from the ranks, as they were privileged to do, and refused to be mustered into said service. They accordingly were dropped from the rolls of the company, from that date.

THE END.

PAPERS

REMINISCENCES.

COMPANY K we presume, was not far behind the general run of soldiers, in "stirring up the de'il."

Many amusing incidents might be recorded, but we give only a few Reminiscences in these pages, as they readily occur to us.

———— • ————

WHO STOLE THE DUMPLINGS?

AT Fairfax Station, Lieut's Minnigh and Kitzmiller having secured some very fine apples, and a batch of real wheat flour, concluded to have an Apple-dumpling dinner. A Camp-kettle was brought into requisition, the dumplings were made by "Cornelius", who took charge of the preparation, and soon the kettle was steaming over a blazing fire.

A few guests were invited, the board was well spread and all waited anxiously, the summons to the feast, for 'Nelius had said, "Dey's most biled, Boss." Suddenly while thus waiting, Cornelius at one bound sprung into the tent and blurted out these words, "deed and double, dey's gone, sure 'nuff; somebody's done gone and stole de dump-l-i-n-e-s, kittle and all!"

This proved to be an actual fact, and to this day the real thief, who stole every-thing but these officer's tremendous appetite for dumplings, has never been discovered.

NO TWO SHOTS,
EVER STRIKE THE SAME SPOT?

INCIDENT at Spottsylvania, will easily be recalled to memory. In some movement, in which our regiment participated, our flank was brought in range with a rebel battery, when a 20 pound shot came whizzing along. Fortunately, it was poorly aimed, and exploded as it struck the ground.

The shell tore a hole in the ground, about ten feet from our line, immediately in front of our company, sufficiently deep to bury a team of mules. Several of the boys said, "No two shots, ever strike the same spot," as they jumped into the cavity, considering it a safe place. Scarcely had they entered it however, until another shot from the same gun, came rico-cheting in the track of the former, struck the ground and tore its way right through under them. The shell did not explode, fortunately, and no one was hurt, but such a "scrabbling out" of that hole, and scratching of dirt out of eyes and ears, was rediculously amusing.

TWO FRIENDS PART FOREVER.

WAS AMUSING to listen to Bill Mumper express himself under the excitement of Battle, when somehow, though brave as a lion, he lost control of himself.

At North Anna river, after we had crossed at Jericho fording, we lay in an open field, and the artillery were throwing shot and shell, to and fro, over our heads. One of the shells exploded prematurely right above us, and a portion coming straight down, struck Mumper's tin-cup buckled to his haversack, which was slung over his shoulder, smashing it into a shapeless mass. Bill got mad, and in his anger uttered words, something like these, "Make out a requisition for a new tin-cup, quick; d——d if that was'nt the last tin in the brigade;" then taking the relic in his hand, he soliloquized as follows.

"Good bye! old tin-cup, Good bye! You've been a faithful friend to me, ... I have'nt time to shed any tears just now, but I'll miss you like ———, and I'll often think of — " Just then a shell exploded right in our midst, and springing to his feet, as the order, attention! was given, he exclaimed finally, "H —— they won't let me alone in my sorrow!"

AN AWFUL DEATH.

A T Charles' City cross roads, when lying down under the heavy cannonry, a solid shot struck a tree, twenty feet from the ground, cutting it off clean from the main trunk. It then dropped to the ground in an upright position, and in doing so, struck the prostrate form of a soldier, lying at the root of the tree, crushing him into the ground. The tree as it impaled the luckless soldier, rose thirty feet into the air, and stood upright by the parent stock.

"SNAP" IN A PIG-PEN.

THE MARCH toward Washington, after the Second Bull-Run, 'Snap' Rouzer got tired out, and concluded to take a rest. Finding a convenient pig-pen by the roadside, he crawled in, and soon was asleep. When he awoke from his slumbers, the troops were still going by, but he resolved, first, to take a look at outside surroundings. When he did so, he discovered that our troops had disappeared, and the Johnnies were going by with long and hurried steps, so he laid low for two mortal hours watching and counting the rebels passing.

When the way was clear, he lit out, by a flank movement and rejoined the company, first reporting to Division Head-quarters, the numbers of the enemy he had seen in pursuit of our forces. He said that a commission was promised him for the valuable information, but the commission never came to hand.

Rouzer frequently was absent from the command, a day or two at a time, and when interrogated as to the matter, would merely say that he had been on a scout.

WE MUST here relate, one of Rouzer's pranks. An order had been issued, from Head-quarters, requiring all soldiers to remain with the Camps of the various regiment, as many were accustomed to pitch their tents in a convenient woods, away from the camp. Jim was one of those affected by the order, but as usual, paid no attention to it, and with several comrades remained out, "where wood and water was plenty." When told of the order, on coming to the main camp for rations, he simply uttered a single bad word, gave his long black mustache a push to one side, (you remember that mustache, one side up in the air and the other trying to look respectable?) and then he went back to his "dog-tent" in the woods.

Presently an officer was sent from Head-quarters, to drive all stragglers into camp, and riding up to Snap's tent, with the usual big fire in front of it, inquired of Jim sitting composedly by the fire, why he was not in camp according to orders. "Well, Captain! I'd like to be there, but I'm taking care of them fellers in there, just now," said Jim, pointing to the tent, where two men were sleeping on a pallet of straw. "This is a hos-pit-tal, and them poor sojers is awful bad with the Small-pox." It is said that the officer concluded that he had business some where else just then, and rode off at full speed, and left Rouzer master of the situation.

"You can't spit in my ear."

HE COMRADES will remember the squad of new recruits, at Camp Tennally, a few of whom were "raw, very raw," but who at the end of the term of service, "were sharp as any."

L——h was one of these, and it is said, some the boys played the following trick on him, when, for the first time, he was put on guard duty. He was warned by the boys, to be a little watchful, as they often played tricks on the new beginners, and named some rediculous things that had been formerly played on recruits, none of which, had any foundation in fact. L——h had no idea that the boys were putting up a job on him, and when put on guard, he walked his beat as proud as a gobbler in a barn-yard, and with an air about him that said, "you can't play any tricks on me!"

About sunset the officer of the camp guard made the rounds, and gave the countersign, whispering the same in the ear of each guard as customary. The officer approached L——h for this purpose, but was held back by a movement of the bayonet, and with a knowing grin, he exclaimed, "Oh! You can't spit in my ear."

A PRINTING PRESS, is an agent by the use of which, much good or much harm may be done, but our object is to preserve a few reminiscences, which ought to be handed down to our children.

Jacobs was on guard, at Regimental Head-quarters on one occasion, and as was often the case when the relief seemed to be behind time, he called out two or three times, very distinctly, "Two o'clock, and no relief." This annoyed Col. Roberts who was awaked in the midst of his slumbers, so when the sentinel again yelled, "Two o'clock, and no-o-o-o — " he never finished, for two distinct shots of a revolver, in the Col's tent attracted his attention, and approaching the same he hurriedly inquired "Colonel, Colonel! any thing the matter, in there?" The reply was, "I did'nt hit you, did'nt I? Now you holler again, d —— you, and I'll blow out your brains." Jacobs did'nt holler any more.

HAVING been detailed for duty, with the Pioneer Corps, he reported at once to Head-quarters, and when they asked his name and regiment, replied "Co. K., of the First, and my name is John Henry Kelley Jacobs." The Captain looked at him inquiringly, and said, "I want only your name, not all the names in the regiment." That was, however, his real name.

IS RELATED that on the march, through Maryland, Rouzer came straggling into camp and reported to the boys, that he had discovered an Ice-house well filled, and not a great ways off. A party of half a dozen, soon were on the way piloted by Jim. Presently, they came to the house, mostly under ground, by the side of a pond of water. The door being locked a few lusty blows knocked it off the hinges, and sure enough, it was well filled, and covered nicely, with a layer of straw. Well, several of the boys jumped in at the same instant, when, Lo! what seemed to be a body of Ice, was water, with a mass of floating straw on top, and the boys were plunging and snorting in six feet of ice-cold, filthy drainage. They charged Snap with a put-up job, and — well, maybe it was.

ORDERLY YOUNG says, that after returning to our camp from the Burnside "stick in the mud," he was ready for almost anything, and that night he and John Brandon played their first game of cards.

By the way, Sammy, where did you play the final game, Hey?

WHO KILLED THAT CALF?

N A FORAGING Expedition, two members of the company found a fatted calf, in a farmers barn-yard, and soon the greater portion of it was transferred to their haver-sacks, and they rejoined the com-mand just in time for the evening Dress-parade.

They kept very quiet about the matter, and no one suspected what was about to happen. The parade was formed the foragers were in the rear rank. After the usual manual of arms, the Colonel gave the command, "Rear rank, open order, March!" this movement be-ing gracefully performed, the Colonel went to the head of the regiment, and accompanied by a citizen, they passed down the line, the farmer scanning the face of every soldier in the front rank; having reached the left of the line, they turned and gave the same atten-tion to the rear rank. Just then, a movement took place in Co. K., two men quickly exchanged places in the rear rank with two others in the front rank, no one outside of the company, it seems, noticing the movement.

The sequel, to the whole proceeding was this. That
lank looking farmer had followed the men into camp,
and having reported to Colonel Roberts, he was told,
that if he could point out the two men, he would have
them punished ; hence the inspection that took place.

Well, he did'nt find the men, but still he said that
they belonged to the First regiment. Of course they
did, but they outwited the farmer.

———— • ————

"SHUNKA–FLIESH."

AN APPETITE for smoked meat, was
omnipresent among the men, and
all the "salt horse and sow-belly"
in the commissary, could not sat-
isfy that appetite.

At Bristow station, it was necessary to make a special trip to army
Head-quarters on the Rapidan, for a supply, but our
"little dutchman" took another plan. Going down the
rail-road to the next station, he jumped an open car
loaded with barrels of ham, (he called it shunka-fliesh,)

and as the train neared our camp, he tumbled a barrel off, into a clump of bushes by the road-side. Then quietly, assisted by others, it was brought into camp.

That was good ham, as we have reason to know, a fine slice having somehow found its way to our table.

--------- • ---------

McCABE'S BIG KNAPSACK.

APTAIN Minnigh at Spottsylvania, was placed in charge of some men, with orders to find the ammunition train, and get a supply of cartridges for the regiment.

The train was soon found, and at no great distance from the command, but the direct intervening space, was open ground and covered by a rebel battery; this necessitated a long detour, in order to reach the regiment in safety. One of the detailed men was McCabe of Co. D, (I think,) a noble and good-hearted specimen of an Irish soldier, and a man who always carried a mule's load in his knapsack; when therefore, each man had shouldered a box of cartridges and started, McCabe turned to the Captain, and said, "Faith and be-jabers Cap'n, an' oi'm goin' shtraight over to the rigament.'' Suiting his action to the words, he was gone.

All went well till he reached the middle of the open space, when the boom of a single gun was heard, and a hissing shell came down the ravine as if it was hunting for the Irishman. He looked around for an instant, then turned just in time to let the shell strike squarely, the well packed knapsack. It knocked him down, his cap going one way and the box of cartridges the other way ; to our surprise he scrabbled up, picked up his cap and deliberately put it on his head, then shouldered the ammunition box, and started again. The fact is, he was not hurt in the least degree. That tremendous knapsack saved his life.

WE witnessed a strange sight on one occasion, as we awoke from the slumber of the night. It was a biv-ouac, and snow had fallen during the night, and as one soldier after another, rose, from under the bed of snow, we thought of the great resurrection morning.

BROKE THE REBEL'S ARM.

THE Battle of Charles' City cross roads, many Charges were made, and many rebel prisoners taken, when an order was given to take no more prisoners, but to disarm them and let them go. After a certain charge, Orderly sergeant Minnigh when the recall was sounded, met **M. M. Miller** returning to our line with two prisoners.

He called Miller's attention to the orders, and said he should smash the muskets around a tree and let the prisoners go. Mike proceeded to do this, but the fellow resisted and there was quite a scuffle. Sergeant M. watched the contest for a moment, but just then he noticed a movement on the part of the other Johnnie, and saw him in the act of levelling a revolver at Miller. Quick action was necessary, and with a spring and a yell he struck the arm of the rebel, with his clubbed musket, sending the pistol into the air, and breaking the arm midway between the elbow and the wrist. Minnigh picked up the revolver and sent it home afterward as a relic. Miller took the muskets, and destroyed them, letting the prisoners go.

THE Floor in Prince William's C. H. Virginia, among a mass of rubbage, Capt. Minnigh picked up several papers that bear the marks of a past age, both in appearance and subject matter, and as relics of the past we insert one or two in these pages; notice the dates.

George the second by the grace of God of great Britain, France and Ireland; King, Defender of the Faith, &c:– To the Sheriff of Prince William County Greeting — We command you to Summon Thomas Fletcher, to appear at the next Court, on the fourth Monday in December next, to testify and say the truth on behalf of Richard Mathews, in a matter of controversy depending and undetermined between the said Richard and Thomas Garner, and this he shall not omit under the penalty of £100. Witness John Graham, Clerk of our said court the 29th, day of November in the xxvii Year of our Reign.

(The date of this paper is Nov. 29th., A.D. 1756.)

Another Interesting Document.

The Commonwealth of Virginia to the Sheriff of Stafford county greeting : You are hereby commanded to take Charles Carter Esq. Enoch Benson, William Mullen and Benjamin Fichlin, if they be found within your bailiwick, and them fafely keep, fo that you have their bodies before the Juftices of our faid county court, at the Court-houfe of the faid county, on the 2d Monday, instant, ... to anfwer Eli Nichols, & Jane his wife, late Jane Follass, and Rachel Follass, of a plea of Debt for 69,500 ℔s, of Crop Tobacco of Falmouth or Fredericksb'g inspection, Damage £50, current money, ... And have there this writ.

Witnefs Thomas G. S Tyler, Clerk of our faid court, the Seventh day of August 1788, in the 14th year of the Commonwealth.

T. G. S. Tyler. — *C.S.C.*

WHO CAN EXPLAIN?

WE give here, a copy of a document, found among the company papers, that fell into our possesion, when the command came into our hands. We venture (a supposition only,) that the paper refers in some way to what was known as "The company fund," viz: money paid to the company by the commissary department, for rations that were not drawn.

Copy of the Statement.

1862.		Cr.
Jan. 26.	Rec'd of Co. fund . .	$61.75
,, 30.	,, Cash · . . .	.30
Feb. 8.	,, of David Myers . .	.25
,, 13.	,, of Capt &c. for sugar .	.20
,, 22.	,, of Com. Sergt. . .	79.00
Mar. 17.	,, for Bread	1.08
May 6.	,, for month of March . .	51.00
	Total credit	$193.58

1862.		Dr.	
Jan. 27.	Stove . .	$3.00	
Feb. 7.	6 copies tactics . .	4.75	
,, 13.	Sand paper . .	.10	
,, 24.	Ex. on $50 sent to bank	.50	
,, 25.	Stockings . .	.50	
Mar. 17.	Bread . .	13.39	
,, 19.	Brushes and blacking	1.95	
June 8.	2 doz. Blacking . .	1.20	$25.39
	Ballance due the company		$168.19

If my supposition is correct, then, who received the monies and as the expressage is charged, where was it sent, and where is it now? The paper has no signature.

It seems to have been a settlement made after September 1. 1863, as it is written on the back of another document dated at that time.

"DOC" ELDEN and THE "BLACK-LEG."

AN EXPERIENCED Gambler came to the front at a certain pay-day, put up his Tent without opposition from the authorities, and opened a "gambling hell," and a number of the boys were beaten out of their hard earned money by the wily rascal.   Doc was lured into the den, and lost every cent he had in a very few games. He then took a favorable position and watched the gambler closely, and soon discovered the secret of his success, and concluded to beat him at his own game. But how? his money was gone. He approached one of his most intimate friends, (every member of of the company was his friend,) and solicited the loan of $10, candidly revealing the facts, as stated above, asserting in addition, the positive assurance of retrieving his former losses.

At this moment another comrade came in and heard the concluding words, and at his suggestion, each gave Doc $5.oo, and having received the cash, he seemed very grateful, then turning to go he said, "I'll pay you back your money to-night."

In about two hours, he returned to camp, paid back the borrowed money, promptly, and held in his hand quite a roll of green-backs besides. When asked the question, "How did you do it?" he answered with a single word, "Bluffing."

"RED TAPE."

HIS was a Term applied to the lengthy routine, through which all business had to pass, even the minutest affair, went from Company to Regimental, thence to Brigade and Division Head-qrs, for approval, after which it was returned to the place of starting, through the same channel, thus taking much time, which often, under certain circumstances, made applications or petitions, a mere farce.

On one occasion, a comrade received a dispatch informing him of the death of his wife. Having applied for leave to go home, it took two days to get it, and when he got home the wife was already buried.

We insert a boda-fide copy of a paper in our possession, (we have many such papers,) that proves our assertion, concerning the "Red-tape" business. Beyond the above, the document has no significance here.

Camp near Auburn, Va.

October 29., 1863.

Captain :—

I have the honor to request, that the Charges preferred by me against Privates H. H. Jones and H. W. C. Elden, members of Co. K, 1st Reg't, (Inf't) P. R. V. C., and now on file at Head-quarters Division Penn'a Reserves, be withdrawn. These men have been (for the last 20 days) doing duty with their company. Their conduct has always, previous to this offence, been such as becomes good soldiers.

Very Respectfully,

Your Obed't Serv't.

H. N. Minnigh.

To Capt. Auchmuty.   Capt. 1st P. R. V. C.

A. Adj't Gen'l, 3 Div. 5th Corps.   Com'd'g Co, K.

On the back of this neatly folded paper, are recorded the following endorsements, in the order given.

Camp near Auburn, Va.
October 29th, 1863.

A request that the charges against Private Jones and Elden of 1st Inft. P. R. V. C. be withdrawn.

Hd-Qrs, 1st Reg't
Oct. 29th 1863.
Approved and respectfully forwarded,
W. W. Stewart.
Lt-col, Comd'g.

Hd-qrs, 1st Brig, Pa. Res.
3d Div. 5th corps.
Oct. 31, 1863.

Respectfully forwarded with the request that the charges against these men be withdrawn — a sufficient punishment can be had by trial before Regt'l commander.
Wm. Cooper Talley.
Col. comd'g Brig.

Head Quarters Div.
Nov. 2, 1863.

Respectfully returned — The charges against Private Elden will be withdrawn. Private Jones will be tried for the charges preferred.

By command of
Brig. Gen'l Crawford.
Comd'g Div.

J. S. Marquis.
A. A. A. G.

Head Qrs. 1st Brigade.
Nov. 2, 1863.

Respectfully returned — attention called to above.

By command of Col. McCandless.
Wm A. Hoyt.
A. A. A. G.

Meeting friends, amid Scenes of strife.

NTHE ADVANCE toward Gettysburg, (our home,) many incidents worthy of note took place, but we will only give, in this connection, portions of a letter, sent us by I. N. Durboraw, Esq., who tells his experience among the friends and relatives, that surrounded him.

Many of Company K. had like experiences, if they cared to relate them.

"I was with the company on the march to Gettysburg," says comrade Durboraw, "and it was amusing as familliar scenes, persons and faces were presented to our view. Some young ladies whom I recognized, as we passed along, not far from my home, and who were waving their handkerchiefs at the soldiers passing by, gazed at me in amazement as I named them, and as they did not recognize me, inquired, one of another, who that could be that knew them. When we arrived at the home of Serg't Young his own brother Robert came to us, but the Sergeant did not leave the ranks.

While in bivouac, in J. M. Diehl's field, where we halted just before noon on July 2, to get a little rest,

and wait for orders, Robison came to me when cook-
ing my coffee, and told me that Peter Baker, living
near by, wished to see me, so I went to his house, and
after getting something to eat, returned promptly to
the company. Just when I reached the command the
orders were given to fall-in double-quick, and hurriedly we advanced to the Round-tops, obliquing into
position left in front, ... fired two rounds,
when the order 'Forward !' was given, and every man
had to hunt his way as best he could, over, round and
through the bushes, rocks, stones and Plum-run swamp
in the flat below. How the rebels, who were in numbers right in our front as the order to charge was given,
it is hard to tell, but most of them did ; when we got
to the wheat-field the line was halted, and finaly es-
tablished at the stone fence, which is in place today.

I now told Capt. Minnigh I was going home, and
that he should neither say, Yes or No ! I went back to
the place where we had piled our knapsacks, the day
before, but could find neither knapsack nor Creamer
the guard, but looking round I eventually found it in
a quarry on the banks of Rock-creek. I had only three
miles home and soon reached it, only to find it filled
with wounded soldiers, Gen'l Meredith being one of
the number. I slept on the floor that night, and the
next morning, with a knapsack well filled, I returned

to the company. I did not find many of the people in the neighborhood at their homes, and their houses were occupied by skulkers and shuysters absent from their commands. When I got back to the company I shared out the contents of my haversack, and when we marched that night it was empty.

On the march that night I passed through a house by the road-side, and met a number of my relatives, but only said, How d'ye do, and Good bye, and was off again."

"Green Persimmon Pies."

HEATED, BY GOSH! was the exclamation of a certain comrade in an undertone, as he spat out a huge mouthful of fresh baked pie. Well! the explanation is just as follows; two pies had been secured on the march that day from a colored woman, at twenty five cents each, but when the soldier came to sample the pies, he found they were made of green persimmons, and the lower crust was corn-meal. No wonder he tried to use "cuss words," his mouth being ready either to swear or to whistle.

Thirty-two rebels Captured on the Picket-line.

INCIDENT at Spottsylvania may be related here. The Picket line had been driven in, and a detail of forty men, was placed in chage of Captain Minnigh who was merely instructed to re-establish that line, which he was told curved in, bringing the rebel pickets near to our Division Head-quarters. The only portion of our line visible was on the extreme right, at a white house on an elevation of ground. He at once proceeded a short distance to the left, and soon reached Burnside's unbroken line, on its extreme right and at the point where that line was broken off abruptly. From this point to the house referred to, was a distance of half a mile, and this space was to be occupied by the new line. "That woods is full of rebels, and you and your men will be captured if you go in there," was an officers greeting when told of the work assigned to the detail, "It will take a brigade to re-establish the line."

Not the least dismayed, the word of command was given and the advance into the woods was started, in a bee-line for the white house, a glimpse of which was occasionally seen through the trees.

By stationing a picket every twenty five yards, the space could be covered, and this was done, without the least molestation on the part of the enemy, not a rebel being visible. Scarcely was the line re-established, when one of the movements peculiar to this campaign commeneed, and an order came instructing the picket line to fall back, preserving an unbroken line. This was done, and when the movement was completed we counted thirty-two rebel pickets captured on the line.

This question remains to be answered. How did the new line of union pickets cut the rebel line in two places, as evidently it did, without seeing an enemy or firing a shot?

A REBEL GIRL "SPIT IN HIS FACE."

ONLY FOR the Soldiers, none for officers," were the words that met Sergeant **M** —— as he took a cup of water out of a bucket, at a yard-gate, in the neat village of Drainsville while the Pa. Reserves were passing through on a reconnoisance.

An aged lady and two young girls stood by the ves-
sel of water, and one of the girls had spoken the words
quoted above. The Sergeant was about to drink from
the well filled cup, when Gen'l Reynolds riding up to
the gate, said to him, "Sergeant! get me a cup of that
water." He promptly handed the cup, still untouched,
to the General, who drank the water, expressed his
thanks and rode away. Deprived of his drink he now
turned to get another cup for himself, but was met by a
blunt refusal from one of the girls, who said, "You
gave your cup of water to that officer, and you cannot
have any more." His reply to this was, "I'll give my
Brigade commander a cup of water every time, even if
it deprives me of a drink, at the hands of a she rebel."

As he finished this direct language she turned quickly and 'spit' in his face, not once but twice. M——
turned and walked away, but took along the bucket
of water.

———— • ————

WHO were the boys, that took a Piano from the
mansion near Camp Pierpont, and hid it in the barn
among the fodder, previous to its shipment north, at
the close of the war? As the war unexpectedly continued for four years afterward it must have been considerably out of tune.

"THAT'S THE VERY FELLOW!"

HE Army of the Potomac, in one of the advances south-ward, crossed the Potomac at the Berlin ferry, and pushed down through Loudoun valley. The Captain was sick during part of this advance, and we give a strange coincidence which then had its origin, in his own words.

After crossing on the Pontoon bridge I was put into an ambulance, and after proceeding a mile or two, I gave my place in the ambulance to a poor fellow who had sun-stroke, and who seemed more dead than alive. I plodded on as best I could, being some distance in the rear of my command, when Gen'l —— followed by his staff came riding along. He addressed me sharply, inquiring why I was away from my command. I told him of my illness and how I had given my place in the ambulance to the soldier, then, with a contemptible toss of the head he muttered, "A likely story," and rode on. In the evening I caught up, at the camping ground, sick, tired and hungry; but soldiers fare was

entirely unpalatable, and I could not eat it, so I went
to the village close by, (Lovettsville,) determined to
secure something tasteful.   I approached a house at
the outskirts of the town, for the flavor of newly baked
pies had been wafted toward me by the evening breeze
and I decided that a pie, a fresh blackberry-pie, was
just what would suit my case. Knocking at a side en-
trance I was admitted by a young lady, who moved a
convenient rocker and bade me be seated.   Presently
a middle-aged lady entered the room, bearing two
pies, which were added to a number already on the
large dining table opened to its full capacity. Taking
courage I told the woman of my illness and my cra-
ving for home-fare, and that in her motherly good-
ness would she sell me two of those pies? She replied,
that she would like to do so, but that General ——
(the same officer I had met on the march that day,)
had ordered the pies, for himself and his staff officers.

With this she left the room, and then I appealed to
the young lady who seemed to be on my side, but she
stated her inability to reverse the decision made by
her aunt, but added these words as she pointed to the
table, "If I want a pie I take it."   That settled the
matter, and I went to the table, put two pies together,
and with an ordinary stride started for camp, convin-
ced that the two pies were not baked for Gen'l ——.

I got to camp all right, and enjoyed the pies exceedingly, and the whole circumstance was soon forgotten, and perhaps never would have been recalled had not the following incident occurred.

When Company K, had been mustered out at the expiration of the full three years term of service, we returned home, and having closed up all the company affairs, I finally turned toward the residence of my father on the corner of Middle and Washington streets, and entered the door as the bell called to supper, I was ushered into the dining-room, and introduced by my mother as the returned soldier boy, and was shown to a seat at the board, where a number of persons, of both sexes were already seated. Suddenly a young lady, a perfect stranger to me, after staring me full in the face for a moment, with a hearty laugh and a glee-ful clapping of her hands, addressing my mother exclaimed, "Oh, Mrs. M., do you remember I told you about a sick officer taking two pies from aunties dining table, down at Lovettsville, Va?" and without waiting for a reply, pointing her finger in my direction she added "That's the very fellow!" This proved to be the same young lady teaching in Gettysburg, and boarding at my mother's table. We enjoyed that supper, after rehearsing the story of the stolen pies, and when supper was about finished, I got an extra piece of pie.

AN INTERESTING STORY! is the general verdict rendered, where ever I have related the incidents connected with my visit home, on the evening of July 3rd, when the command was relieved from the front, at the Round-tops.

As the Story may be interesting to others, I will relate it for the benefit of all.

When we went into bivouac, on the spot where the Round-top Park dancing-floor now stands, many of the company whose homes were in Gettysburg or the immediate vicinity, quietly slipped away, and believing that our work, for a while at least, was ended, I also went, saying to the boys when I started, "Boys if you go home, don't fail to get back to-morrow morning." I am proud of the conduct of company K, at, as well as after the battle of Gettysburg, and why should I not be? These brave fellow could easily imagine the dangerous surroundings of loved ones, during the terrible conflict, in their homes within the bounds of the battle-field, yet, not a man left the ranks or fled from duty, and while most of them got home after the battle, by a peculiar device, only one failed to return.

But to my story; I passed northward just in the rear of the line of battle, and through the Citizens cemetery, thence up Baltimore street to the Court-house on the corner of Middle street, which was a dangerous performance, as the whole route was exposed to rebel sharp-shooters, making it necessary to cross all streets and alleys at a bound. Having reached the point indicated, I found the residence of my father, on west Middle street one square from the Court-house, so completely covered by rebel sharp-shooters, that it was an impossible measure to go there.

I observed things closely, and saw a certain officer who was apparetly not acquainted with the dangerous surroundings, turn the corner where I was standing, and walk deliberately down in the middle of the street, without being molested, but, Alas! the poor fellow when he got below Washington street, was taken prisoner. So I took advantage of what I had seen, and walked down the street, with misgivings I confess, for doubtless many rifles were aimed at me, with a rebel finger on each trigger, ready to send as many messengers of death, if I should turn either to the right or to the left. It was an awful moment, but I determined to carry out my plan, which was to spring into a flower garden on the east side of the house, when I would reach that point, for I would then be in a safe place.

On! on, to hesitate would be fatal; and how terrible it would be to die so near to the loved ones; still on I went, not hurriedly, for the enemy must not even think that I have a purpose in view; Oh! If only the yard gate were open! Ah, it is open! A spring, and I am through it, and behind the cover of the house ; I am safe, but what a shower of minnie balls strike the pavement over which I came, and how they tear through the palings of the fence on both sides of the open gate, terrible messengers they are, but harmless now as far they concerned me.

None of the family were visible, so I entered the unlocked door of a back kitchen, which was empty, then into the main building I went and all through it from main floor to attic, and found no one ; disappointed I turned to the cellar and was met on the stair-way by a sister, who failed to recognize me in the semi-darkness, who said, "Here! what do you want?" On the spur of the moment I said, "Can you supply me with just a bite to eat?" With this she retired below and I followed to the foot of the stairs, and took a seat near the lower step, and this is what I then saw : father and mother, four sisters and a brother, two or three improvised beds, an almost consumed tallow dip on the end of a barrel in a far off corner, and each person being a perfect image of dejection and despondency.

Sister Lucy whispered something to mother, who then entered an adjoining pantry, doubtless to get the "bite to eat," while a younger sister approached me inquiring, "I wonder how much longer we will have to remain in this cellar?" I merely answered, "Not long," but I discovered that they were entirely ignorant of the state affairs without. She looked at me closely, and then followed mother into the pantry.

Presently, mother approached me, bearing a huge piece of bread in her hand, and peering very closely into my face, then as if in glad surprise, she ejaculated, "Oh, you bad fellow, I know you now! Here's your supper."

I will not attempt a portrayal of the scene that followed, but in a few words I revealed the state of affairs without, and brought them from that lower world, in which they had dwelt several days, into the light and comfort of the upper world once more.

Soon an ample supper spread the board, and then all retired to the comfortable beds, of which they had been deprived for two nights, and I had not enjoyed for two years. That night the confederate army began the evacuation of Gettysburg.

Lieut. Sadler, buried at home.

THE 14th of September 1862, at South Mountain, in the charge up the last acclivity, and just when the victory was won, Lieut. J. D. Sadler fell in death, and Lieut. Minnigh was wounded.

As I wish to relate the circumstances connected with the removal of Sadler's body from the field where he fell, to his home fifty-two miles away, for burial, and as I in my wounded state, in the face of many difficulties in the way, undertook the work of removal, I will tell the story, in my own words.

I was wounded by a minnie ball, through the left arm near the shoulder, when in the act of crossing the stone fence at the foot of the hill, and as my arm dropped to my side being completely paralyzed, I believed the injury was greater than it afterward proved to be, hence, I did not proceed any further. Having retired to the field hospital, a surgeon grasped my wounded arm and after a cursory examination, said, "Your arm must be taken off," but I did not see things just in that light, and slipped away.

At Middletown, four miles away, dwelt a relative of my wife's family, Appelman by name, and Mrs. A., was at the same time Lieut. Sadler's aunt, so I determined to go there. Upon reaching the village I was informed, that Dr. Reed our Regimental surgeon, was in charge of the Gen'l Hospital in a Church, so I went there. He told me my arm was all right after removing quite large piece of the bone.

-After mid-night, I found the home above indicated, but as no response came to my timid rapping, I waited for the morning. At the early dawn I was admitted to the house, got a good breakfast, had my arm dressed and was put to bed. Presently voices were heard below stairs, and I recognized that of Roades of our company. Hastening below I heard the sad news of Lieut. Sadler's death, as well as the other losses that befel the company. We at once planned the removal of his body by private conveyance, to York Springs, Pa., a distance of fifty-two miles.

Mr. Appelman had two horses in his stable, and we concluded to use them in the furtherance of our plans. A hearse and driver were secured, and Sadler's body was brought from the battle-field, en-coffined, and all things got ready for an early start on the morning of the Sixteenth; I determined to accompany the body incognito, and borrowed a citizens suit accordingly.

On the morning of the 17th at 2 o'clock, we started
with the hearse drawn by one horse, and I mounted
on the other horse, apparently the most unsophistoca-
ted countryman you ever saw. Let me say here, that
I had determined to accompany the body, and as it
would have been impossible to have secured a leave of
absence, the above measure was adopted, so as not to
be annoyed by the Provost guard.

We soon reached Frederick city and passed through
unmolested, but at a toll-gate a mile out on the Emmittsburg pike we found the out-posts, who refused to
let us pass, but after giving satisfactory answers to all
questions, we finally were permitted to pass on. At
Creagerstown we fed our horses and took breakfast, I
also resumed the military uniform, as there was now
no necessity of a disguise. Near the town of Emmittsburg I stopped at a residence, in the front yard of
which there was a well of water, for the purpose of ba-
thing my wounded arm, when a woman came rushing
out and said, no Union soldier could have any water
from that well; I answered in laughing good humor,
that I thought I knew one who would, when she took
hold of the pump handle. and tried to prevent my
pumping the water. I gently pushed her away, when
she called a dog to her assistance, and a large blood-
hound rushed around the house, and sprung at me.

But I was ready, and a single shot laid him low. At this, the woman commenced to cry bitterly, and said she would call the men; my reply was, that the men would be dealt with in the same way. No men appeared fortunately, and I mounted my horse and rode off.

At Emmittsburg we fed our horses and took dinner, and then we were on the road again. A few miles out on the Gettysburg road we were met by my father and brother, who came with a conveyance to aid me on my way. We reached Gettysburg about 4 o'clock, and rested until after supper, and then were off again, having still 14 miles to the end of our journey. But I was entirely worn out, when I reached Heidlersburg. I went into the hotel, kept by a relation of Sadler, threw myself on a bar-room bench, and —— slept, slept so soundly that I could not be awakened, so they carried me to bed, and I was surprised next morning, to find myself there and still seven miles to the journey's end.

After breakfast, I quickly covered this distance, and found all arrangements made, for the funeral that day in the afternoon. A squad of raw material, was briefly drilled, in the manual of arms, and at 4 o'clock, we buried "our fallen comrade" with the honors of war, in the family burial ground, at Hampton, to await the reveille on the morning of the resurrection day.

In Memoriam.

OUR FALLEN COMRADES!

Killed in Battle.

J. F. Bailey, Charles City cross roads, June 30, 1862.
J. D. Sadler, South mountain, Sept. 14, 1862.
P. W. Miller,   ,,   ,,
Jere. Nailor,   ,,   ,,
J. W. Shipley, Spottsylvania, May 18, 1864.
C. F. Wisotzkey, Mechanicsville, June 26, 1862.

Died of Wounds.

Wm. McGrew, at Field hospital, July 6, 1863.
J. J. Duey,   ,,   date not known.

Died in Prison.

H. W. C. Elden, at Florence, Ala. date not known.

Died of Disease.

J. F. Creamer, Mt. Pleasant hosp't, Dec. 21, 1863.
F. A. Keim, Hosp't, Baltimore, Md. no date.
J. W. McKinney, Alexandria, Va. Feb. 24, 1863.
G. W. Myers, at Camp Pierpont, Dec. 3, 1861.
Jesse Shank,   ,,   Nov. 24, 1861.

IT WOULD be in vain for me to attempt a proper Eulogium, of the character of these fallen heroes. They gave up the fair promise of a useful life, gave up chances of fame, aye! gave up life for the Salvation of the common country. In what light can I set the high mark of their patriotism? What words can tell the story of their courage, with what language can I adorn their lofty heroism?

How valiently they fought, how serenely and sublimely they died.

They fell in the fierce conflict. amid the cheers, the fire, the smoke, the flame, soothed in the dying hour by the consciousness that victory came to side of right and truth and liberty, and that "Old Glory" still waved triumphantly. They have pitched their tents, in the eternal bivouac beyond the stars, and are camped in the mysterious and unknown silence of the life immortal.

Oh, unconquerable heroes! Let it never be said that the great republic is forgetful of your deeds, or unmindful of those whom you most loved.

Finally, my Comrades, let us fight valiently, on all the stern battle-fields of this life, so that, when the last tattoo is beaten, and 'lights out' forever, we shall be worthy to join the immortal ranks of the comrades on the other side, and march before the Great Reviewing officer, when time and earth and hostile armies are no more forever.

THE END.